Foundations and Frontiers in Decision Science - Theory, Methods and Applications

Edited by Dakshina Ranjan Kisku

Published in London, United Kingdom

Foundations and Frontiers in Decision Science - Theory, Methods and Applications
http://dx.doi.org/10.5772/intechopen.1008092
Edited by Dakshina Ranjan Kisku

Contributors
Annapurna Singha Roy, Chang-Jing Ji, Eyüp Akçetin, Louis B. Rosenberg, Mark Klein, Nurhayat Çalışkan Akçetin, Satish Kumar, Vanita Rani, Xiang-Yu Wang, Xiaodan Wang

First published in London, United Kingdom, 2026 by IntechOpen

IntechOpen is the global imprint of INTECHOPEN LIMITED, registered in England and Wales, registration number: 11086078, 167-169 Great Portland Street, London, W1W 5PF, United Kingdom

For EU product safety concerns: IN TECH d.o.o., Prolaz Marije Krucifikse Kozulić 3, 51000 Rijeka, Croatia, info@intechopen.com or visit our website at intechopen.com.

British Library Cataloguing-in-Publication Data

A catalogue record for this book is available from the British Library

Foundations and Frontiers in Decision Science - Theory, Methods and Applications
Edited by Dakshina Ranjan Kisku
p. cm.
Print ISBN 978-1-83634-197-0
Online ISBN 978-1-83634-196-3
eBook (PDF) ISBN 978-1-83634-198-7

Meet the editor

Dr. Dakshina Ranjan Kisku is an Associate Professor in Computer Science & Engineering at NIT Durgapur, India. He holds a BEng, an MEng, and a Ph.D. (Computer Science & Engineering) from Jadavpur University, and an MS in Data Science from the University of East London. With 22+ years of experience, he specializes in Biometrics, Data Science, Image Processing, Computer Vision, Machine Learning, and Deep Learning. He has authored/edited five books, published over 150 peer-reviewed articles, and holds two granted patents in public healthcare. Recipient of the IEI Young Engineers Award and many notable accolades, Senior Member IEEE, Fellow RSPH (London), Fellow IEI (India), Principal Member of the BIS Biometrics Committee, and External Expert for ISO. Currently guiding Ph.D. scholars and leading Vision Systems research at NIT Durgapur.

Contents

Preface

Decision science stands at the intersection of human reasoning, social science, philosophy, data, and technology, guiding us through choices that shape our personal lives, organizations, and societies. In an era marked by rapid digital transformation, climate challenges, and ethical dilemmas, understanding how we make decisions and how we can improve them has never been more vital. *Foundations and Frontiers in Decision Science – Theory, Methods and Applications* brings together diverse perspectives from leading scholars to explore the field's core principles while pushing its boundaries into new territory. As the editor of this volume, I am delighted to present a collection that bridges relevant theories with cutting-edge innovations, providing valuable insights for researchers, practitioners, and students alike.

This book explores the dual nature of decision-making, examining the intuitive and analytical processes that drive our choices, as highlighted in the opening chapter, "Perspective Chapter: Decision Science in the Digital Age – Integrating Theory and AI-Enhanced Decision-Making" by Annapurna Singha Roy. Her work examines how decision science integrates economics, psychology, and data science in the digital age, addressing challenges such as cognitive biases and ethical issues in AI-driven decision-making. She introduces the 5C Hybrid Decision Framework as a tool to harmonize human judgment with machine intelligence.

Building on these foundations, Nurhayat Çalışkan Akçetin and Eyüp Akçetin explore the philosophical foundations of decision science. Their chapter, "Perspective Chapter: Philosophical Boundaries of Decision Science – Unknowability, Uncertainty, and the Quest for Meaning", questions assumptions of pure rationality, weaving in concepts from cognitive psychology, behavioral economics, and ethics to emphasize uncertainty, free will, and the search for meaning. It calls for a human-centred approach that values humility and collective well-being.

The volume then turns to the role of artificial intelligence in scaling human collaboration. Mark Klein, in his chapter "How Can AI Help Achieve Effective Deliberation at Scale?", discusses how large language models (LLMs) can enhance group deliberation by overcoming barriers through techniques such as content unbundling, creativity cueing, and stakeholder analysis. His insights reveal promising ways for humans and AI to partner in solving complex problems.

Louis Rosenberg extends this theme by introducing a chapter, "Collective Superintelligence: Enabling Real-Time Conversational Deliberations among Humans and AI Agents at Unprecedented Scale", a technology inspired by natural swarms, such as bee hives and fish schools. This chapter demonstrates how CSI enables real-time discussions among unlimited groups of humans and AI agents, thereby amplifying collective intelligence to address open-ended challenges.

Shifting to real-world applications, Chang-Jing Ji, Xiaodan Wang, and Xiang-Yu Wang apply decision science to carbon emission reduction in their chapter, "Decision Science for Carbon Emission Reduction: Integrating Systemic Frameworks and Emerging Technologies". They outline hybrid methodologies that combine predictive analytics, behavioral insights, and emerging technologies to tackle climate change, while stressing the need for ethical and sustainable frameworks to pursue a net-zero future.

Finally, the book addresses advanced quantitative tools with a chapter "Distance Measure between Intuitionistic Fuzzy Sets with Its Application to TOPSIS and Decision-Making Problems". This work proposes a novel, non-linear measure that improves accuracy in multi-attribute decision-making problems, such as those using the TOPSIS method, and demonstrates its superiority through practical examples.

Together, these chapters reflect the evolving landscape of decision science, from theoretical and philosophical roots to practical frontiers in AI, social science, environmental policy, and fuzzy logic. They remind us that effective decisions require not just data and algorithms, but also understanding, ethics, and innovation. I extend my gratitude to the contributors for their thoughtful work and to the readers who will carry these ideas forward.

I hope that this book will serve as a valuable guide, illuminating the ongoing evolution of decision science and inspiring further research and practice in this vital area.

Dakshina Ranjan Kisku
Department of Computer Science and Engineering,
National Institute of Technology Durgapur,
Durgapur, India

Chapter 1

Perspective Chapter: Decision Science in the Digital Age – Integrating Theory and AI-Enhanced Decision-Making

Annapurna Singha Roy

Abstract

Decision-making is a critical component of existence influenced by both intuitive (fast) and analytical (slow) thinking, as explained through the dual-system argument. This is how decision science relates itself to the disciplines where economics, psychology, and data science converge in improving the act of making choices in business, healthcare, and government policymaking. Important theories, such as decision theory, have also been reviewed in light of digital advancements. Although data-driven decision-making increases accuracy and efficiency, uncertainty, cognitive biases (such as the framing effect), and ethical dilemmas in AI-based decisions continue to pose challenges. Advances in human-AI collaboration and computation are putting their print on the future of decision science and promising new balances between automated insights and human judgment. Examples of techniques to counteract biases and thus improve decision quality would include data analytics, emotional intelligence, and mindfulness. The 5C Hybrid Decision Framework is presented in the study as a way to balance machine intelligence and human judgment. But it also points out that some of the biggest problems facing digital decision systems are those related to prejudice, ethics, and transparency.

Keywords: decision science, artificial intelligence, machine learning, human-AI collaboration, cognitive bias, data-driven decisions

1. Introduction

1.1 Overview of decision science in the digital era

Decision science is a multidisciplinary field that combines *economics*, *psychology*, and *data science* to enhance decision-making processes across various domains. By examining both *intuitive* and *analytical* thinking, it helps explain how individuals and organizations make choices under conditions of uncertainty. The integration of these two cognitive modes, as articulated in the *dual-system theory* [1], highlights the complex interplay between human judgment, biases, and rational analysis, especially when supported by advanced computational tools and data-driven insights.

This version incorporates a bit more *depth* by emphasizing the role of *computational tools* and the *human-AI interaction* that is becoming increasingly important in decision science.

Figure 1 illustrates how decision science is an interdisciplinary field that integrates key concepts from economics, psychology, and data science. From economics, it adopts principles such as risk and reward, as well as cost-benefit analysis, to support rational decision-making. Psychology contributes insights into cognitive biases and emotional intelligence, which affect how individuals make choices. Data science enhances the process through AI integration and data-driven analysis. At the intersection of these disciplines, decision science aims to develop comprehensive decision-making theories that balance human behavior with analytical and technological tools. There are several sophisticated computational tools introduced by the digital era. They include decision support systems, predictive analytics, and machine learning algorithms. These technologies have helped organizations process enormous data volumes in real time, providing far more accurate and scalable decision-making processes than the older human-centric way [2, 3]. Therefore, traditional decision science approaches have evolved from theoretical frameworks to hybrid models that integrate intuition with automated analysis in making decisions [4, 5]. This development, however, has not been without its own challenges. Although AI-based systems are efficient and consistent, they come with their own important issues of transparency, accountability, and ethical governance [6, 7]. Besides the algorithmic bias and overreliance on automation, a lack of human interpretability may lower the standard of decision quality and diminish social trust, especially in high stakes such as healthcare and finance or public policy

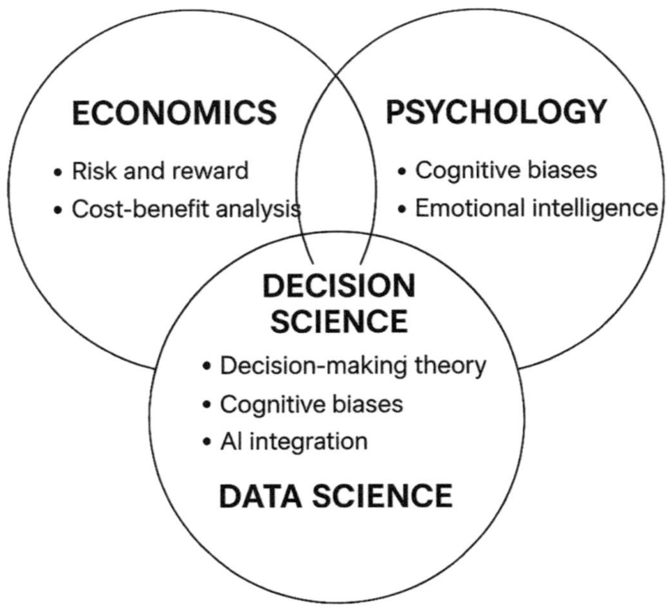

Figure 1.
The decision science structure.

decision-making [6, 8]. Besides that, recently in some areas, around the interdisciplinary decision making has gradually started seeing the active applications of economic, psychological, and data science paradigms so as to improve the utility and ethical standards of AI-driven systems.

Moreover, emerging strategies such as emotional intelligence training, mindfulness practices, and advanced data analytics are being explored to reduce bias and enhance decision-making quality in high-pressure digital environments.

2. Literature review

Decision science has become a vital discipline for understanding and enhancing decision-making, particularly in the domain of digital transformation. Previous studies allow us to draw some inferences about human cognition, technological tools, and decision-making frameworks interacting in such processes:

2.1 Dual-system theory

According to Kahneman's [1] perspective, System 1 thinking is intuitive, while System 2 is analytical. Such a duality is considered central to studying decisions made under uncertainty and time pressure.

2.2 Behavioral biases in decision-making

Various studies (e.g., Dietvorst et al. [7]) have proved that biases prevent individuals from trusting algorithmic decision-making, such as algorithm aversion, even though algorithms are usually better than humans at making decisions.

2.3 Human-AI collaboration

According to Jarrahi and Raisch and Krakowski [5, 8], there should be a collaborative model where AI acts to support human judgment rather than replace it. The hybrid system is promising in reducing human cognitive limitations while ensuring its ethical accountability.

2.4 Digital decision tools

Decision support systems and predictive analytics are transforming traditional models. Shrestha et al. [4] have investigated the restructuring effect of digital tools on the organizational decision framework from a classical hierarchical viewpoint to data-centric organizational forms.

3. Theoretical framework

3.1 Proposed theoretical framework: The 5C hybrid decision framework

In an increasingly complex and digitized sphere, ever more so in decision-making practices today, we propose a new integrated framework called the 5C Hybrid

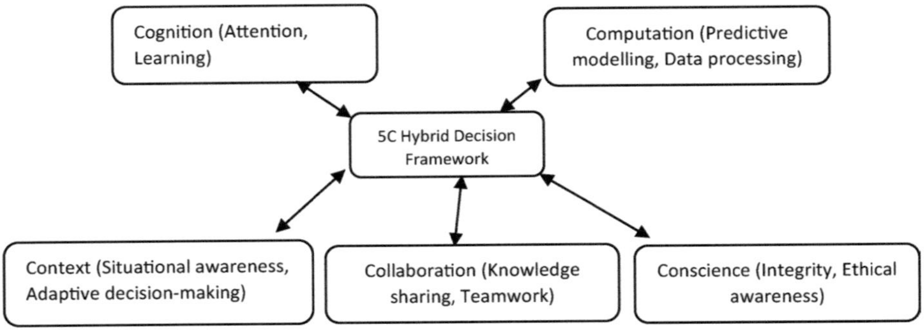

Figure 2.
Proposed theoretical framework: The 5C hybrid decision framework.

Decision Framework. This framework is an amalgamation of cognitive theory, computational power, contextual sensitivity, collaborative intelligence, and ethical conscience, which together forge an integrated structure toward a higher quality in decision-making (**Figure 2**).

3.2 Overview of the 5C components in decision framework

See **Table 1**.

Cognition	From the dual-system theory, this component highlights the interaction between fast-intuitive thinking and slow-analytical thinking while making decisions.
Computation	Responses include any form of technical procedures, such as AI, algorithms, machine learning, and big data analytics, to gain insight, reduce errors, and enhance efficiency.
Context	Assuming environmental, social, and organizational factors that can influence decisions in a given domain (e.g., healthcare, business).
Collaboration	Maintaining a working and intellectual relationship bridging human and machine logic, as well as synergizing an interdisciplinary collaboration among roles (e.g., data scientists, strategists).
Conscience	Considering all ethical interests in the decision-making process, thus assuring fairness, accountability, and transparency in decisions that are automated or assisted.

Table 1.
Core elements and their functional roles in the 5C hybrid decision framework.

3.3 AI-assisted decision-making process

A generalized framework for AI-assisted decision-making includes the following. steps:

1. Data collection: Gather relevant data from various sources.

2. Data preprocessing: Clean and organize data for analysis.

3. Model training: Develop ML models using historical data.

4. Prediction generation: Use trained models to make predictions or classifications.

5. Decision support: Present predictions to human decision-makers with confidence levels.

6. Human oversight: Humans review AI recommendations, applying domain knowledge and ethical considerations.

7. Feedback loop: Incorporate outcomes to refine models continuously.

The machine learning pipeline is shown in **Figure 3** with its application in real life, say, for healthcare. Data collection is the initial step, involving the gathering of pertinent information such as patient records, medical histories, and lifestyle particulars. Then comes data preprocessing, whereby the data are cleansed and structured for analysis to eliminate inconsistencies in the dataset. Once the data are set, training occurs: algorithms internalize data to detect patterns, such as assessing the probability of a patient developing a specific disease. Human evaluation is applied at this stage to assess the model's behaviour for ethical and accurate outcomes. The next stage of training is activation, wherein the model begins producing outputs given new input data and is leveraged in decision support to assist health professionals in providing treatment solutions. A feedback loop is also set up so that real-world outcomes can be gratefully fed back into the system to aid further refinement and improvement of the model. Basically, the cyclical nature of the procedure means the system will continue to become more accurate and viable with use.

3.4 Real examples of AI/ML in decision-making

Recent research work has shown that ML and AI have been used effectively in improving decision-making in different scenarios. For example, a randomized controlled trial has provided evidence of AI-assisted decision-making: pharmacists who performed verification of prescription fills with assistance from uncertainty-aware AI rejected wrong prescriptions more accurately (96.1%) than those assisted by black-box AI models (91.8%) or those who decided without AI assistance (81.2%) [9]. In other contexts, Oxford has developed an AI tool, named Lizzy, to assess the risk of domestic abuse from victim responses. This AI tool reached an

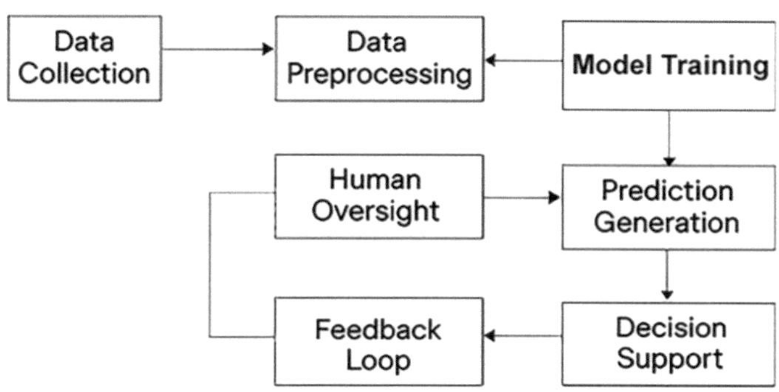

Figure 3.
AI decision-making process.

84% accuracy level—better than all traditional instruments—and hence contributed toward a 50% reduction in repeat domestic abuse in some areas [10]. In addition, the Valencia region in Spain applied AI to handle the crisis by analyzing anonymized mobile data and surveys to track the spread of the virus and the level of public sentiment. An AI-based approach to forecasting the infection peaks effectively gave way for resource allocation and public health measures and immensely enhanced the response to the pandemic in the region [11]. These examples illustrate the transformative impact of machine learning (ML) and artificial intelligence (AI) on decision-making, enhancing its speed, accuracy, and overall effectiveness across various industries.

4. Impact of digital technologies on decision science

The digital epoch has immensely ameliorated the discipline of decision science with AI, ML, and big data analytics so as to improve decision-making, lessen human prejudices, and generally operational efficiencies. These technologies serve both System 1 (intuitive) and System 2 (analytical) decision-making processes, according to the dual-system theory [1]. In business systems, for example, AI forecasts demand and segments customers, thus strategically enabling managers in better decision-making through the data [12]. In the healthcare sector, ML models can aid in early diagnosis and treatment recommendations by processing complex information, such as patient histories and genomic data, thereby contributing to improved clinical decisions [12]. In public policy and governance, AI tools forecast crime patterns or traffic flows by utilizing real-time data from IoT sensors, highlighting the evolution of digital systems toward actionable, real-world decision-making [13]. Human-AI symbiosis is appearing as the next battleground, with humans providing ethical oversight and contextual understanding, whereas machines supply speed and scale in execution. This interaction serves to reduce cognitive biases and increase the accuracy of decisions [14]. Ethical concerns, transparency of the algorithm, and data privacy issues remain to be addressed and demand well-thought-out frameworks for producing trustworthy and fair digital decision systems [15].

5. Challenges in digital decision-making

While digital technologies promise to be transformative in decision science, several challenges stem from their ethical, transparent, and reliable use. These challenges need urgent attention if digital decision-making is to be responsibly upheld in industries such as business, healthcare, and governance.

1. *Algorithmic bias and discrimination*: There is also an ethical issue since existing social inequalities are perpetuated or, in some cases, worsened when machine learning models are trained on biased or incomplete datasets [2]. For example, a paper found that a healthcare algorithm implemented in various hospitals across the United States systematically assigned lower risk scores to Black patients than to White patients with similar health conditions, such that access to care was limited for the former set of patients. AI-based decisions are thus confronted with these biases in fairness and inclusivity.

2. *Lack of transparency (Black Box System)*: A large number of AI systems behave like black boxes, giving out outputs without explaining how decisions have been arrived at. In high-impact domains, such as finance, recruitment, or criminal justice, this lack of transparency becomes a threat to establishing accountability [4]. Without such explanations, how can any user or regulator audit the decision or, in fact, even trust it?

3. *Data privacy and security concerns*: Digital decision-making heavily relies on personal and behavioral data, raising critical issues related to privacy, user consent, and cybersecurity. These concerns are particularly relevant in the context of Zuboff's "*The Age of Surveillance*," which highlights how extensive data collection can lead to ethical and societal challenges.

6. Case studies in data-driven system

Case study: Enhancing hospital capacity management through data-driven decision support.

6.1 Overview

In response to the challenges posed by fluctuating patient volumes, particularly during the COVID-19 pandemic, the Johns Hopkins Health System implemented an interactive decision support dashboard. This tool integrates real-time hospital data, predictive analytics, and optimization models to assist administrators in making informed decisions about hospital capacity management [16].

6.2 Key features

- *Real-time data integration*: The dashboard integrates data from different hospital systems and presents current status information about bed occupancy, staffing levels, and availability of resources.

- *Predictive analytics*: Using historical data and machine learning algorithms, the system forecasts patient admission rates and potential surges in demand for taxes and other resources.

- *Optimization models*: It uses optimization techniques to advise the most efficient allocation of patients and resources across the hospital network.

- *User-centric*: Developed with inputs from hospital administrators, the dashboard's user-friendly interface allows users to run various scenarios and explore potential outcomes.

6.3 Impact

The deployment of this dashboard led to improved decision-making during critical periods, ensuring optimal utilization of hospital resources and enhanced patient care. Its success underscores the importance of integrating data analytics into healthcare operations.

6.4 Outcomes and impact

- Improved decision-making: enabled quicker, more data-informed decisions during crisis periods.
- Reduced overcrowding: helped distribute patient loads evenly across the health system, preventing ICU saturation.
- Proactive planning: allowed administrators to simulate various scenarios and prepare for potential surges.

6.5 Broader implications for decision science

This case highlights the power of integrating decision science, AI, and data visualization in real-world healthcare. It illustrates how System 2 thinking (analytical reasoning) is enhanced through digital tools while also requiring human judgment to interpret model outputs ethically and contextually.

7. Opportunities and emerging trends

Nowadays, irreversible decision sciences have obtained a soul and an essence, citing disruptive tools and methodologies through which decisions could be developed more easily. Human-AI collaboration systems ensure that machines support, rather than usually replace, human judgment. Explainable AI promotes algorithmic explanation, which, in turn, supports transparency and trust. Real-time data analysis equips users with the tools for fast and rightly informed decision-making in a slightly dynamic environment. Emotion-aware systems have started tinkering with the response according to user behavior and sentiment. Ethical frameworks are advancing to make sure all technology is used responsibly. These trends signal the growth of smarter and more adaptable human-centered decision systems.

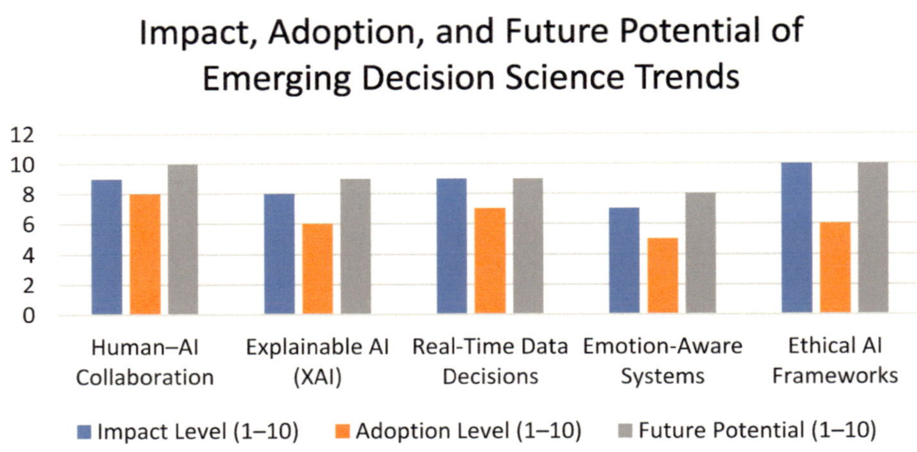

Figure 4.
Analysis of five key decision science trends based on their current impact, level of adoption, and future potential (on a scale of 1–10).

A comparative evaluation of emerging trends in digital decision science was conducted based on synthesized insights from recent research and expert consensus [15, 17, 18]. The evaluation focuses on three factors: current impact, adoption level, and future potential. **Figure 4** chart highlights that human-AI collaboration and ethical AI frameworks show the highest potential for the future impact of decision science. Explainable AI and real-time decisions are rapidly growing in adoption. These trends collectively reflect a strong shift toward transparent, intelligent, and human-aligned decision systems.

8. Conclusions

Going with the Uncle Ken style of thought, this article examines how traditional views of decision-making from a cognitive perspective (such as Kahneman's dual-process theory) are challenged by recent computational advances in each decision-making scenario of the different domains. The 5C Hybrid Framework—Cognition, Computation, Context, Collaboration, and Conscience—is an umbrella model under which the challenges and opportunities of AI-assisted decisions can be discussed in useful terms. The advent of predictive analytics, real-time dashboards, and explainable AI technologies underscores the importance of ensuring that the speed of the machines can be harnessed by prudent judgment from the human side. Algorithmic bias, transparency, and data privacy issues continue to be the key areas of concern. Healthcare and public policy case studies point to the greater potential that ethically based, data-driven decision support systems hold. As we see the rise of trends such as human-AI collaboration and emotion-aware systems, decision science will become a globetrotting interdisciplinary research field with an emphasis on the human part. In pursuing this goal, nurturing additional innovations with an ethical and contextual mind will be imperative if juxtaposed digital decision-making is to prove constructive in designing responsible, accurate, and transparent decision systems.

Author details

Annapurna Singha Roy
Nopany Institute of Management Studies, Kolkata, India

*Address all correspondence to: annapurnasroy@gmail.com

References

[1] Kahneman D. Thinking, Fast and Slow. Straus and Giroux: Farrar; 2011

[2] Brynjolfsson E, McAfee A. The business of artificial intelligence: What it can – And cannot – Do for your organization. Harvard Business Review. 2017. Available from: https://hbr.org/2017/07/the-business-of-artificial-intelligence

[3] Davenport TH, Ronanki R. Artificial intelligence for the real world. Harvard Business Review. 2018. Available from: https://hbr.org/2018/01/artificial-intelligence-for-the-real-world

[4] Shrestha YR, Ben-Menahem SM, von Krogh G. Organizational decision-making structures in the age of artificial intelligence. California Management Review. 2019;**61**(4):66-83. DOI: 10.1177/0008125619862257

[5] Raisch S, Krakowski S. Artificial intelligence and management: The automation–augmentation paradox. Academy of Management Review. 2021;**46**(1):192-210. DOI: 10.5465/amr.2020.0106

[6] Binns R. Fairness in machine learning: Lessons from political philosophy. In: Proceedings of the 2018 Conference on Fairness, Accountability, and Transparency. New York, NY, USA: Association for Computing Machinery (ACM); 2018. pp. 149-159. DOI: 10.1145/3287560.3287598

[7] Dietvorst BJ, Simmons JP, Massey C. Algorithm aversion: People erroneously avoid algorithms after seeing them err. Journal of Experimental Psychology: General. 2015;**144**(1):114-126. DOI: 10.1037/xge0000033

[8] Jarrahi MH. Artificial intelligence and the future of work: Human-AI symbiosis in organizational decision making. Business Horizons. 2018;**61**(4):577-586. DOI: 10.1016/j.bushor.2018.03.007

[9] Preprints.jmir.org. The impact of AI assistance on pharmacists' decision-making: A randomized controlled trial. 2020. Available from: https://preprints.jmir.org/preprint/64902

[10] The Times. AI can help police predict if someone is at risk of domestic abuse. 2020. Available from: https://www.thetimes.co.uk/article/ai-can-help-police-predict-if-someone-is-at-risk-of-domestic-abuse-jbbrbgt9m

[11] Wired. How valencia used AI to track and manage COVID-19. 2020. Available from: https://www.wired.com/story/valencia-ai-covid-data

[12] Obermeyer Z, Emanuel EJ. Predicting the future — Big data, machine learning, and clinical medicine. The New England Journal of Medicine. 2016;**375**(13):1216-1219. DOI: 10.1056/NEJMp1606181

[13] Lee I, Lee K. The Internet of Things (IoT): Applications, investments, and challenges for enterprises. Business Horizons. 2015;**58**(4):431-440. DOI: 10.1016/j.bushor.2015.03.008

[14] Amershi S et al. Guidelines for human-AI interaction. In: Proceedings of the 2019 CHI Conference on Human Factors in Computing Systems. New York, NY, USA: Association for Computing Machinery (ACM); 2019. pp. 1-13. DOI: 10.1145/3290605.3300233

[15] Mittelstadt BD et al. The ethics of algorithms: Mapping the debate.

Big Data & Society. 2016;**3**(2):1-21. DOI: 10.1177/2053951716679679

[16] Raisch S, Krakowski S. Artificial intelligence and management: The decision-support dashboard for optimal hospital capacity management. arXiv preprint. 2024. arXiv:2403.15634. Available from: https://arxiv.org/abs/2403.15634

[17] Brynjolfsson E, McElheran K. The rapid adoption of data-driven decision-making. American Economic Review. 2016;**106**(5):133-139. DOI: 10.1257/aer.p20161016

[18] Ribeiro MT, Singh S, Guestrin C. "Why should I trust you?": Explaining the predictions of any classifier. In: Proceedings of the 22nd ACM SIGKDD International Conference on Knowledge Discovery and Data Mining. New York, NY, USA: Association for Computing Machinery (ACM); 2016. pp. 1135-1144. DOI: 10.1145/2939672.2939778

Chapter 2

Perspective Chapter: Philosophical Boundaries of Decision Science – Unknowability, Uncertainty, and the Quest for Meaning

Nurhayat Çalışkan Akçetin and Eyüp Akçetin

Abstract

Decision science is predominantly known for its quantitative methodologies and rational models designed to optimize human and organizational choices. This study, however, elucidates the fundamental philosophical frontiers that shape decision science, focusing on the interplay of unknowability, uncertainty, and the human search for intrinsic meaning. Questioning the assumptions of pure rationality and the limitations found in traditional decision models, this writing draws upon foundational and contemporary literature from cognitive psychology, decision theory, behavioral economics, and ethics. The discussion demonstrates how cognitive biases, limited information, and uncertainty fundamentally affect the decision-making process, while integrating philosophical perspectives such as existentialism and pragmatism to emphasize the role of free will, ethical frameworks, and human values. The text concludes with a call to action to integrate human-centered principles into decision-making practices, fostering an approach that embraces humility, flexibility, and a commitment to the collective good.

Keywords: decision science, philosophy, limitations, ethics, rationality, uncertainty, unknowability, search for meaning, values, decision making

1. Introduction

This study examines the philosophical boundaries of decision science within the framework of a literature review, focusing on the challenges posed by unknowability, uncertainty, and the human quest for meaning. Although decision science offers powerful models for rational choices based on utility maximization, the foundations of these models are challenged by the limits of human knowledge, the unpredictable nature of reality, and the immeasurable aspects of human values. This review synthesizes foundational texts of decision theory, critiques from behavioral economics, and philosophical insights from fields such as epistemology, existentialism, and narrative theory to address these boundaries under three main themes: (1) The Rational Foundations and Cognitive Limits of Decision Science, (2) The Epistemological

Challenge of Uncertainty and Unknowability, and (3) The Quest for Meaning: Axiological and Existential Decisions Beyond Utility and Calculation.

The classical decision-making model, originating from the Enlightenment ideal of the rational actor, serves as the starting point for this discussion. Primarily developed in the fields of economics and statistics, this model assumes that a decision-maker can identify all possible outcomes, assign probabilities to them, and choose the option that maximizes their expected utility. According to this approach, a rational individual should be able to state clearly which of two alternative events they prefer and to extend this comparison to include combinations of events with specific probabilities ([1], pp. 8–28).

This framework is known as Expected Utility Theory (EUT) and has become the cornerstone of rational choice. Leonard J. Savage (1917–1971) extended EUT to situations of uncertainty where probabilities are not objectively known, developing his own subjective expected utility theory and arguing that even subjective beliefs can be structured rationally. This main theory of decision-making under risk is based on a set of axioms defining rational choice, such as the transitivity of preferences, and it predicts that a rational decision-maker will always choose the alternative that provides the highest expected utility ([2], pp. 3–7, 27–31, 73, 105).

2. The rational foundations and cognitive limits of decision science

The first significant challenge to rationality was posed by Herbert Simon (1916–2001) with his concept of Bounded Rationality. Simon argued that human cognitive limitations—incomplete information, time constraints, and computational capacity—prevent decision-makers from maximizing utility. According to him, people "satisfice" rather than "optimize," that is, they seek not the best solution, but one that is acceptable or "good enough." Simon emphasized that the physiological and psychological limits of the organism should be treated as fundamental constraints defining an optimization problem and incorporated into the formulation of the rational choice process ([3], pp. 99–111; [4], pp. 25–26).

Daniel Kahneman (1934–2024) and Amos Tversky (1937–1996), with their pioneering work in behavioral economics, supported Simon's theoretical critique with experimental evidence. Their research demonstrated that human decisions systematically and predictably deviate from EUT. Concepts such as loss aversion, the framing effect, and a series of cognitive heuristics and biases revealed that human "rationality" is not purely logical but is, in fact, deeply psychological and context-dependent ([5], pp. 265–280). For instance, due to the principle that psychological response is a concave function of physical change, "the value difference between a gain of 100 and a gain of 200 appears to be greater than the value difference between a gain of 1,100 and a gain of 1,200" ([5], p. 278). Similarly, perceptual judgments also vary with context; distances are exaggerated in poor visibility conditions, while they are underestimated in good visibility. People are often unaware of the rules that govern such impressions, but they can learn to recognize these biases and make conscious corrections ([6], p. 1125).

These findings have shown that the psychology of the decision-maker can be more decisive than the mathematical purity of the model. Simon himself suggested in a later work that such phenomena are better explained not by concepts like "the cost of thinking," but by prospect theory and framing analysis ([7], p. 458). Consequently, the existence of systematic biases and intuitive preferences that consistently violate the rules of rational choice in human decisions has been accepted. While valid intuitions can be developed with expertise, unfortunately, the intuitions of professionals are not always based on true expertise ([8], p. 15, 17).

2.1 The landscape of cognitive biases and their philosophical implications

Decision-making is a fundamental action continuously performed by humans and is therefore a focus of many disciplines, including mathematics, economics, psychology, and sociology. Decision studies address both normative questions (related to rationality and logic) and descriptive questions (related to how people actually make decisions), and the tension between these two perspectives constitutes the core dynamics of the field ([8], p. 504).

Cognitive biases, representing systematic deviations from rational judgment, reveal the inherent fallibility of human reason. The classic work of Tversky and Kahneman identified numerous biases, such as the anchoring effect (where initial information has a disproportionate influence on subsequent judgments) and the availability heuristic (where the probability of more vivid or memorable events is overestimated). These biases demonstrate that human cognition is not perfectly rational and that real-world decision-makers operate within a complex interplay of conscious analysis and subconscious influences. From a philosophical standpoint, this resonates with existentialist thought, which emphasizes the unpredictability of individual choice and the layered complexity of human subjectivity. Acknowledging the pervasive nature of these biases forces decision science to recognize the inherent limitations of human judgment and to question the adequacy of models built solely on rationality ([9], p. 209).

3. The epistemological challenge of uncertainty and unknowability

The challenges facing decision science do not end with the limitations of the human mind. The very nature of the reality from which information is obtained also presents a fundamental epistemological challenge: Is the world knowable enough for rational models to work effectively?

Frank Knight (1885–1972) made a foundational distinction in this area, positing a philosophical separation between risk and uncertainty. Risk refers to situations where outcomes are unknown but their probability distributions are known, whereas uncertainty describes situations where these probability distributions are themselves unknown or unknowable. Standard decision models can effectively manage risk, but they fundamentally fail in the face of true "Knightian uncertainty" ([10], pp. 230–232). According to Knight, society and civilization are built upon an accumulation of material, intellectual, and moral capital from the past, and radically altering this complex structure is exceedingly difficult, especially given our ignorance about what we truly want. This highlights the deep uncertainty inherent in large-scale decisions ([10], p. 375).

Practical proof of this philosophical distinction can be seen in the Ellsberg Paradox, which shows individuals' tendency to prefer situations with known probabilities (risk) over those with unknown probabilities (uncertainty), even if the outcomes are equivalent ([11], pp. 650–655). This situation, identified by Ellsberg, points to the existence of a powerful psychological tendency known as ambiguity aversion, which distorts rational utility calculation. Ellsberg argued that people do not always assign probabilities to uncertain events and may deliberately violate the axioms of rational choice in such situations. While questioning whether this behavior is irrational, he notes that he is among those who behave this way:

> *"Does it leave any room, then, for a concept of 'unmeasurable uncertainty': of uncertainties that are not 'risks,' not subject to numerical or even qualitative probabilities? (...) I propose to indicate a class of choice-situations in which many otherwise reasonable people neither wish, nor tend, to conform to the Savage postulates, nor to others that have been devised. (...) Are they foolish? It is not the object of this paper to judge. (...) In any case, it is no business of a descriptive theory to judge them so summarily: I am one of them. (...) They violate the axioms deliberately, without apology, because it seems to them the sensible way to behave. Are they clearly mistaken?" ([11], pp. 646, 668–669)*

Nassim Nicholas Taleb (1960–) radicalizes this view with his concept of the "Black Swan." Taleb argues that our world is governed by rare, high-impact events that are unpredictable from past data. From this perspective, decision models based on historical data are not only limited but also dangerous, as they create a misleading sense of control and predictability. Our cumulative forecasting errors in political and economic events are so vast that what is surprising is not the magnitude of our forecasting errors, but our unawareness of it. This becomes even more concerning when we enter into deadly conflicts. Wars are fundamentally unpredictable. Because Black Swans are unpredictable, we need to adjust to their existence ([12], p. 23).

Taleb states that people often confuse rare events with periodic ones ([12], p. 280) and label things they cannot predict as "random," not due to the nature of the process, but simply because of their own lack of knowledge ([12], p. 309). According to him, the world we live in is full of feedback loops where events cause more events, creating snowball effects that make the planet unpredictable ([12], p. 25). These "Black Swan" events are often labeled as "exogenous" because they fall outside the scope of the models, and the failure of the models is thus rationalized ([12], p. 152).

Similarly, Karl Popper's (1902–1994) principle of falsifiability also undermines these probabilistic foundations. Popper suggests that one can never achieve absolute certainty about the future based on past observations because no matter how much evidence supports a theory, a single future counter-observation is sufficient to refute it ([13], pp. 16–21). "An empirical system must satisfy one other condition besides being consistent: it must be falsifiable. (...) Statements which do not satisfy the condition of falsifiability cannot differentiate between any two statements within the totality of all possible empirical basic statements" ([13], pp. 72–73).

As a practical response to these philosophical problems, institutions like the RAND Corporation have developed the concept of Deep Uncertainty. This concept refers to situations where decision-makers do not know, or cannot agree on, the system model, the probabilities, or how to value the outcomes. For such situations, instead of trying to find an "optimal" solution for a single projected future, methods like Robust Decision Making (RDM) have been proposed. RDM, as a pragmatic response to the problem of unknowability, aims to find flexible and adaptive strategies that perform well across a wide range of possible futures. "The robustness criterion is admirably suited for the discovery of useful policy arguments that are valid over multiple plausible futures" ([14], p. 55). "People learn. They get new information over time. Accordingly, adaptive decision strategies are the most frequently used tool to provide robustness, because they are designed to evolve in response to new data" ([14], p. 57). RDM aims to find flexible and adaptive strategies that perform well across a wide variety of possible futures.

This confrontation with an uncertain world, which resists full probabilistic capture, naturally shifts the basis of decision-making from calculation to the axiological and existential frameworks required to navigate it.

4. The quest for meaning: Axiological and existential boundaries

It is precisely on this ground of unknowability, where probabilities and calculations fall short, that the next dimension of human decisions comes to the forefront: the quest for meaning and value. Perhaps, the most profound limitation of decision science lies in its inability to respond to the human need for immeasurable purpose, value, and narrative. Beyond the cost-benefit calculations of rational models, human decisions are shaped within an existential, moral, and narrative context.

Existential philosophy lies at the core of this critique. For thinkers like Jean-Paul Sartre (1905–1980), choice is not about maximizing utility but about the individual creating their own essence. The human being, "condemned to be free," creatively defines themself in an ultimately meaningless universe with every choice. The emotion accompanying this radical freedom, which cannot be captured by quantitative decision models, is anxiety (Angst). According to Sartre, anxiety does not arise from the unknowability of an underlying determinism; on the contrary, anxiety is the very consciousness of freedom and therefore cannot be invalidated by the assumption of psychological determinism ([15], p. 13).

Addressing this existential theme from a different direction, Martin Heidegger (1889–1976) argues that the fundamental problem of the modern technological age is the dominance of a way of thinking he calls "calculative thinking" (rechnendes Denken). This mindset, constantly focused on monitoring, controlling, and optimizing, reduces the world and even people to a stock of resources to be managed and used—what Heidegger calls the "standing-reserve" (Bestand). In this process, the essential bond between man—the only being who can question the meaning of Being—and being is severed. The self-accelerating development of technology surpasses human will and decision-making capacity, leaving the individual "defenseless and helpless" before this power. As an antidote, Heidegger proposes developing "meditative thinking" (besinnliches Denken), a deeper form of thought that questions the meaning behind our existence. According to him, abandoning this meditative capacity in favor of mere calculation turns a person into a "man of the technological age" ([16], pp. 14–18). Paradoxically, Heidegger does not demand the rejection of technology but a deeper understanding of its essence. Confronting the essence of technology in this way brings forth a liberating claim that saves us from blind technological determinism and returns us to our authentic being ([17], pp. 27–33, 68–69).

These philosophical critiques find a concrete echo in the observations of psychiatrist and Holocaust survivor Viktor Frankl (1905–1997). Frankl argued that the fundamental human drive is not pleasure, but the "will to meaning." He observed that even in the most challenging conditions, people made decisions to survive by attributing meaning to their suffering. Frankl emphasizes that such decisions transcend simple cost-benefit analyses. "Man is not one thing among others; things determine each other, but man is ultimately self-determining. What he becomes—within the limits of endowment and environment—he has made out of himself. In the concentration camps, for example, in this living laboratory and on this testing ground, we watched and witnessed some of our comrades behave like swine while others behaved like saints. Man has both potentialities within himself; which one is actualized depends on decisions but not on conditions" ([18], p. 157).

According to Frankl, it is impossible to judge a person who chooses one thing over another in ultimate matters like life and death, because "No man should judge unless he asks himself in absolute honesty whether in a similar situation he might not have done the same" ([18], p. 68).

This quest for meaning is also supported by moral philosophers who suggest that individual decisions should be placed within a broader narrative framework. Alasdair MacIntyre (1929–2025) advocates for a return to a teleological understanding of morality, where actions and decisions are judged by their coherence with the narrative of a "good life." According to him, decisions are not isolated events but points in a life story, and their goodness depends on their alignment with the individual's ultimate purpose (telos) ([19], pp. 95–96, 104, 156). This moral and narrative dimension also brings with it criticisms of the fundamental assumptions of utilitarianism. Elizabeth Anderson (1959–) criticizes utilitarianism for reducing diverse values (respect for persons, appreciation of art, etc.) to a single metric of utility, arguing that this reduction commodifies values [20]. Similarly, philosophers like İoanna Kuçuradi (1936–) question the utilitarian basis of decision science by emphasizing that the "rightness" of decisions is related not only to the utility of the consequences but also to the moral value of the actions themselves [21].

Even historical anecdotes, such as the perception of David Hume's (1711–1776) deathbed skepticism as insincere by observers, demonstrate the complexity of human meaning and belief and how it resists simple logical inference ([22], p. 248). Consequently, decision science falls short in the face of these rich and immeasurable dimensions of human experience.

5. Reflections of philosophical boundaries in modern decision systems

These philosophical, moral, and existential dimensions find concrete reflections in modern systems, especially where technology is increasingly integrated into decision processes.

5.1 Limitations of modeling and simulation

Critiques of technical approaches often arise from the practical limitations of modeling and simulation. Although these tools have revolutionized decision-making by providing precise and quantitative insights, they inherently fail to capture the full spectrum of reality and human experience. No matter how comprehensive, models are inevitably based on simplifying assumptions about the complex and unpredictable nature of reality.

Elements such as cognitive biases, contextual effects, and intrinsic uncertainties resist full quantification. These limitations become particularly apparent in situations where models fail to accurately account for rare or unexpected events—"Black Swans" in Nassim Taleb's terms. Consequently, one of the main criticisms of quantitative models is their over-reliance on historical data and rigid assumptions, which can inhibit true innovation in the face of new emerging challenges.

5.2 Artificial intelligence, ethics, and trust

The philosophical boundaries discussed in the preceding sections become particularly prominent in Artificial Intelligence (AI)-assisted decision-making systems. While AI is a powerful tool that can complement human knowledge, it clearly shows that the human decision-making process is not merely an optimization problem. Studies show that people frequently deviate from AI recommendations, even when accuracy rates are comparable. This proves that decisions are influenced by factors beyond accuracy or efficiency, such as autonomy, trust, and meaning. In this context, the cognitive biases identified by Tversky and Kahneman regain critical importance for understanding human cognition in AI-supported environments. These biases can lead individuals to construct subjective realities based on perception rather than objective input, distorting judgments, and it is imperative that these effects are also analyzed in AI-assisted decision-making processes ([23], p. 2).

These philosophical and psychological dimensions reveal the importance of integrating ethical considerations into modern decision systems. Recent studies show that incorporating philosophical and ethical frameworks into decision-making processes yields more balanced outcomes, especially in fields like health, finance, and technology. Integrating ethics requires not just adding a layer of moral reasoning to existing technical models, but reframing the act of decision-making itself. For example, in AI development and deployment, decision scientists must strike a delicate balance between algorithmic performance optimization and ethical consequences. In this vein, Woodgate and Ajmeri advocate for macro-ethical principles that ensure not only algorithmic efficiency but also respect for broader human values such as fairness, accountability, and transparency.

Two main categories of principles have emerged in the AI ethics literature:

1. *Ethical principles* derived from normative ethics (e.g., Deontology and Consequentialism).

2. *AI keystones* adapted from fields like medicine and bioethics, which include concepts such as beneficence, non-maleficence, autonomy, justice, transparency, and accountability. These keystones should form the foundation of AI technology design ([24], p. 3).

Case studies in technology sectors show that systems embodying these philosophical and ethical dimensions tend to gain more user trust and sustainable adoption compared to those based solely on deterministic algorithms ([25], pp. 647–650). Transparency plays a critical role in building this trust. Two types of transparency are particularly effective: explaining the algorithmic processes and clearly communicating the AI's reliability. While it may not always be possible to understand complex AI decision mechanisms, transparency about the system's capabilities and expected reliability helps calibrate user expectations with actual performance. This can reduce unrealistically high initial trust levels and stabilize trust over time. Indeed, studies have shown that informing users about an agent's true reliability increases both trust and performance ([25], p. 638).

Furthermore, the dynamics of human-AI trust are highly complex. Since laboratory conditions can artificially inflate initial trust, field studies in real-world settings, such as organizations where AI is already used in management or decision systems, are critically important. Therefore, more research is needed in areas where the use of AI carries personal risk for users ([25], p. 647).

6. Synthesis and conclusion: Towards a holistic decision science

Decision science is a field where we explore its philosophical frontiers, moving beyond its rational and quantitative foundations. This study identifies three fundamental challenges that shape the decision-making process: the *cognitive limit*, arising from the structural constraints of human reason; the *epistemological limit*, stemming from the unpredictable nature of reality; and the *axiological/existential limit*, which originates from the search for value and meaning that lies at the core of the human experience.

These limits are not a failure of decision science, but rather an invitation to understand its human dimension. Decision-making is not merely the act of calculating optimal utility, but also of taking a stand in the face of uncertainty, defining our values, and creating a meaningful life narrative.

In light of this synthesis, our analysis confirms the existence of three distinct yet interconnected frontiers for the field of decision science:

The cognitive limit: Grounded in the work of Simon, Kahneman, and Tversky, this frontier confirms that human rationality is bounded and systematically influenced by cognitive biases. Decision-making is not a purely logical process but a deeply psychological and contextual one.

The epistemological limit: Drawing from Knight and Taleb, this limit highlights the fundamental distinction between manageable risk and true uncertainty. The existence of unpredictable, high-impact "Black Swans" reveals that models based on historical data are inherently fragile and can create a dangerous illusion of control.

The axiological/existential limit: This most profound limit, informed by existentialism and ethics, argues that human choices are often driven by an immeasurable quest for meaning, value, and narrative coherence that transcends utilitarian calculations. Decisions are not merely about optimizing outcomes but about defining who we are.

In summary, the three distinct philosophical frontiers for decision science are as follows:

The cognitive limit: Human rationality is bounded and subject to systematic biases. *The epistemological limit*: The world is characterized by genuine uncertainty and unknowable "Black Swans" alongside manageable risks. *The axiological/existential limit*: Human decisions are driven by an immeasurable search for meaning, value, and narrative coherence that transcends the logic of utility.

In conclusion, decision science remains an invaluable tool for structured problems and conditions of risk. However, its philosophical limits become apparent when faced with complex situations involving deep uncertainty, cognitive constraints, and the human search for meaning. A more holistic and "humble" approach to decision-making requires integrating the analytical rigor of decision science with the wisdom of philosophy and the humanities.

6.1 Policy recommendations and future research directions

In light of the philosophical frontiers discussed in this article, several recommendations emerge for both future research and policy formulation:

Future research: Studies should continue to develop dynamic models that capture the complexity of uncertainty and unknowability, while also integrating qualitative methods that account for ethical and existential factors in human decision-making. Priority should be given to interdisciplinary research that bridges the gaps between quantitative techniques and normative evaluations. Specifically, research should focus on: the dynamic modeling of uncertainty, the ethical implications of AI-assisted decision-making, the integration of quantitative and qualitative methodologies, and a deeper understanding of cognitive biases.

Policy recommendations: Policymakers should mandate the integration of ethical oversight mechanisms into decision-making processes, especially those involving AI systems. Regulations should be informed by interdisciplinary research and ensure that decision systems not only optimize for performance but also adhere to principles of fairness, accountability, and respect for human dignity. Institutions can establish ethical review boards to identify potential biases.

Educational initiatives: Academic programs and professional development courses in decision science should include modules on philosophy, ethics, and cognitive psychology to prepare future leaders for the complex challenges of contemporary decision-making. Decision-makers across various sectors should be trained not only in quantitative methodologies but also in ethical reasoning and cognitive bias awareness.

These research directions and policy interventions will contribute to the evolution of a decision science paradigm that is robust, flexible, and imbued with a commitment to the collective good. Acknowledging that the most important choices in life are often the ones that cannot be calculated is the first step in this evolution.

In conclusion, although the rational actor model constitutes an important foundation in decision science, its cognitive, epistemological, and existential limits show that it does not possess universal explanatory power. To fully grasp the complexity of human decisions, it is imperative that these philosophical dimensions are also included in the analysis.

Author details

Nurhayat Çalışkan Akçetin* and Eyüp Akçetin
Mugla Sitki Kocman University, Mugla, Turkey

*Address all correspondence to: nurhayatakcetin@mu.edu.tr

References

[1] Von Neumann J, Morgenstern O. Formulation of the economic problem. In: Theory of Games and Economic Behavior. 60th anniversary ed. Princeton, NJ: Princeton University Press; 2004. pp. 1-45. (Original work published 1944)

[2] Savage LJ. The Foundations of Statistics. Rev. ed. Mineola, NY: Dover Publications; 1972. (Original work published 1954)

[3] Simon HA. A behavioral model of rational choice. The Quarterly Journal of Economics. 1955;**69**(1):99-118. DOI: 10.2307/1884852

[4] Simon HA. Bounded rationality in social science: Today and tomorrow. Mind and Society. 2000;**1**(1):25-39. DOI: 10.1007/BF02512227

[5] Kahneman D, Tversky A. Prospect theory: An analysis of decision under risk. In: Gärdenfors P, Sahlin N-E, editors. Decision, Probability, and Utility: Selected Readings. Cambridge, UK: Cambridge University Press; 1988. pp. 183-214 (Reprinted from "Econometrica," 47 (1979), pp. 263-291). DOI: 10.1017/CBO9780511609220.014

[6] Tversky A, Kahneman D. Judgment under uncertainty: Heuristics and biases. Science. 1974;**185**(4157):1124-1131. DOI: 10.1126/science.185.4157.1124

[7] Tversky A, Kahneman D. The framing of decisions and the psychology of choice. Science. 1981;**211**(4481):453-458. DOI: 10.1126/science.7455683

[8] Kahneman D. Hızlı ve yavaş düşünme (F. Deniztekin and O. Ç. Deniztekin, Trans.). Istanbul, Turkey: Varlık Yayınları; 2017

[9] Tversky A, Kahneman D. Availability: A heuristic for judging frequency and probability. Cognitive Psychology. 1973;**5**(2):207-232. DOI: 10.1016/0010-0285(73)90033-9

[10] Knight FH. Risk, Uncertainty, and Profit. Boston, MA: Houghton Mifflin; 1964. New York: Augustus M. Kelley

[11] Ellsberg D. Risk, ambiguity, and savage axioms. The Quarterly Journal of Economics. 1961;**75**(4):643-669. DOI: 10.2307/1884324

[12] Taleb NN. The Black Swan: The Impact of the Highly Improbable. New York, NY: Random House Publishing Group; 2007

[13] Popper KR. The Logic of Scientific Discovery. London, England: Routledge; 2002 (Original work published 1959)

[14] Lempert RJ, Popper SW, Bankes SC. Shaping the Next One Hundred Years: New Methods for Quantitative, Long-Term Policy Analysis. 1st ed. Santa Monica, CA: RAND Corporation; 2003. Available from: http://www.jstor.org/stable/10.7249/mr1626rpc

[15] Sartre J-P. Being and Nothingness: An Essay on Phenomenological Ontology (H. Barnes, Trans.). New York, NY: Philosophical Library; 1956

[16] Heidegger M. Olmaya Bırakılmışlık (M. Keskin, Trans.). İstanbul: Avesta; 2013

[17] Heidegger M. Teknik ve Dönüş (N. Aça, Çev). Ankara: Bilim ve Sanat Yayınları; 1998

[18] Frankl VE. Man's Search for Meaning: An Introduction to Logotherapy (I. Lasch, Trans.). Baston: Beacon Press; 1992

[19] MacIntyre A. After Virtue: A Study in Moral Theory. 3rd ed. Notre Dame, IN: University of Notre Dame Press; 2007

[20] Anderson E. Value in Ethics and Economics. Cambridge: Harvard University Press; 1993

[21] Kuçuradi İ. Etik. Ankara, Turkey: Türkiye Felsefe Kurumu; 2018

[22] Noxon J. Hume's agnosticism. The Philosophical Review. 1964;**73**(2):248-261. DOI: 10.2307/2183340

[23] Rastogi C, Zhang Y, Wei D, Varshney KR, Dhurandhar A, Tomsett R. Deciding fast and slow: The role of cognitive biases in AI-assisted decision-making. arXiv. 2020:1-22. DOI: 10.48550/arXiv.2010.07938 [Preprint]

[24] Woodgate J, Ajmeri N. Normative ethics principles for responsible AI systems: Taxonomy and future directions. arXiv. ACM Computing Surveys. 2022;**56**(11):1-37. DOI: 10.48550/arXiv.2208.12616

[25] Glikson E, Woolley AW. Human trust in artificial intelligence: Review of empirical research. Academy of Management Annals. 2020;**14**(2):627-660. DOI: 10.5465/annals.2018.0057

Chapter 3

How Can AI Help Achieve Effective Deliberation at Scale?

Mark Klein

Abstract

This paper discusses how our research group is using AI, particularly LLMs, to help collectives of humans achieve effective deliberation at scale.[1] This paper, in particular: (1) identifies the *goals* that scalable deliberation should ideally achieve, (2) enumerates the *barriers* that frequently get in the way of achieving these goals, (3) proposes *solutions* for overcoming these barriers, informed by our analysis of the relative strengths and weaknesses of humans and LLMs at performing deliberation tasks. The solutions we report in this paper include such concepts as content unbundling, content restatement, creativity cueing, argument structure advising, clustering, participant modeling, and stakeholder analysis. We report current results for implemented solutions when we have them and, in other cases, present ideas that we are in the process of turning into reality. In doing so, we hope to broaden researchers' images of how they can help achieve effective scalable deliberation at scale, as well as give participants and facilitators a better sense of what the future may hold in terms of how they deliberate in partnership with AI systems.

Keywords: collective intelligence, crowd-scale deliberation, AI, LLMs, structured collective decision-making

1. Introduction

The goal of this paper is to systematically explore how AI, particularly LLMs, can help us achieve effective deliberation at scale. In the following sections we will:

- discuss why deliberation at scale is so *important*
- present a *normative model* of what "ideal" deliberations should achieve (goals)
- *identify the weaknesses* in the technologies we currently use (barriers)
- describe how our research group is working to *overcome these weaknesses* (solutions)
- discuss *lessons learned* and propose possible *next steps*

[1] By "scale" we mean, large in terms of the *number* of participants, *complexity* of topics, *extension* in time, and *distribution* of participants in space.

2. The need for effective deliberation at scale

Let us define deliberation as when groups of people try to find solutions for problems they share.

Deliberation processes have changed little in centuries. Typically, individuals or small groups of powerful stakeholders and designated experts craft solutions behind closed doors. No matter how intelligent or well-informed they may be, dealing with increasingly highly complex problems inevitably strains the cognitive capacity of these individuals and leads to sub-optimal decisions.

Most people affected by the decisions, in addition, have limited input during the process, so important ideas and perspectives do not get incorporated. This creates the perception, and often the reality, or self-dealing by the decision-makers. Small-circle decision-making is thus also facing a crisis of legitimacy, squandering the opportunity for broader acceptance and efficient implementation of decisions.

Humanity thus now needs to deliberate effectively about highly complex and contentious problems—such as climate change, security, and poverty—that inherently require integrating the expertise and preferences of tens, hundreds or even thousands of individuals (i.e., *crowd-scale* deliberation). Work in the field of collective intelligence has shown that engaging crowds in deliberation has the potential to solve difficult problems far better than individuals or small groups of experts can. This occurs because of powerful emergent phenomena that include:

- *Many hands*: the advent of cheap digital communication and ubiquitous personal computing has revealed the existence of a massive cognitive surplus: very large numbers of people with deep and diverse skill sets are eager to participate in collective tasks, driven by such non-monetary incentives as contributing to problem or communities they care about [1, 2]. Wikipedia is an excellent example of this.

- *Casting a wide net:* frequently, solutions for difficult problems can be found by consulting outside of the usual small circle of conventional experts [3].

- *Idea synergy:* out-of-the-box solutions can often be achieved by bringing together many individuals and engaging them in *combining* and *refining* each other's ideas [4].

- *Wisdom of crowds:* collectives of suitably diverse, motivated and independent raters have been shown to produce assessment accuracy that exceeds that of experts [5, 6].

- *Many eyes:* our ability to detect possible problems in solution ideas increases dramatically by engaging more people in the task. This has been one of the key reasons for the spectacular success of open-source software [7].

- *Alignment:* engaging stakeholders in making decisions has the great advantage of reducing the resistance and confusion when we try to actually *implement* the solutions developed by the deliberation engagement.

DOI: http://dx.doi.org/10.5772/intechopen.1013039

One of the truly heart-breaking attributes of our current era, however, is that despite the overwhelming *need* for effective crowd-scale deliberation, the vast *potential* of collective intelligence for achieving this, and the existence of the immensely powerful computing and communication *infrastructure* needed to realize this potential, we still frequently come up with solutions whose results almost none of us individually want. Why does this happen, and what can we do about it? We will use, to structure this exploration, a technique known as GBS (goal-barrier-solution) analysis [8]. This will involve enumerating (1) the *goals* that a good deliberation approach needs to achieve, (2) the potential *barriers* to achieving these goals, and (3) the possible *solutions* for overcoming these barriers.

3. Limitations of existing deliberation technologies

The tools we currently use for enabling scalable deliberations (i.e., email, chatrooms, forums, blogs, micro-blogs, and so on), in essence, *move conversations into the digital world*. Their only concern is enabling the exchange of text, speech and images quickly and at global scale. They have become very successful for enabling social connection and knowledge sharing, but how well do they do at enabling scalable deliberation?

3.1 A normative model of scalable deliberation

Any assessment of deliberation technology (as well as any attempt to improve it) must be informed by a model of what a good deliberation approach *should* achieve. The normative model we use for this is based, first of all, on *design thinking* [9–11] which proposes that problem solving should consist of the following stages, which can be presented as a "deliberation diamond" (**Figure 1**).

The stages of design thinking include:

- *Define* the deliberation, i.e., the problem to be solved, the criteria for what represents a good solution, and the crowd needed to work on it.
- *Ideate* possible solutions (often called "divergent" thinking)
- *Critique* the solutions with respect to how well they satisfy the requirements
- *Filter* to find the top candidate solution(s) (often called "convergent" thinking)
- *Select* which of the top-ranked solutions should be implemented

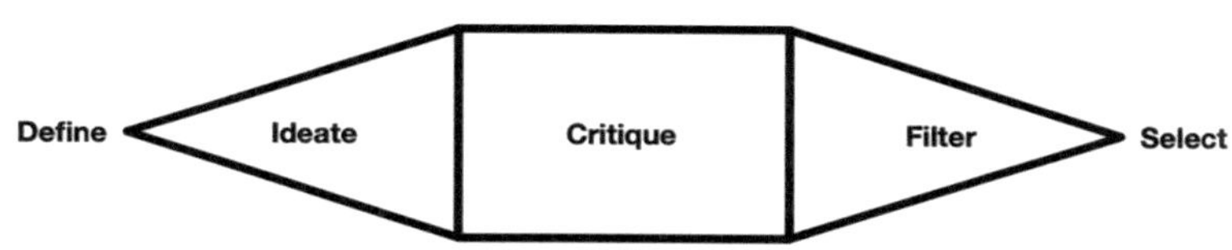

Figure 1.
The stages of design thinking.

Our model then draws from research on collective intelligence to identify what it takes to make design thinking work successfully *at scale.* The key goals for these stages include:

- *Clear problem definition:* Clearly and fully define which questions need to be answered, what the criteria for good answers are, and who should be engaged to work on the problems.

- *Excellent ideation*: Elicit a comprehensive corpus of possible solutions, using the principles of "casting a wide net" and "idea synergy."

- *Comprehensive critiques*: Assess the answers thoroughly and rigorously using the principle of "many eyes."

- *Accurate filtering*: Use the wisdom of the crowd to distinguish good from bad answers by assessing them with respect to the assessment criteria.

- *Correct selection:* Select the best answer(s) to be implemented. The answers should be pareto-optimal (pareto-optimality is a rigorous measure of optimality for decisions where there are multiple decision criteria) [12] and should take into account which stakeholder groups are affected how in order to maximize community alignment and therefore foster successful implementation of the solutions.

In addition to these stage-specific requirements, there are two additional general goals:

- *Maximal efficiency:* The deliberation should progress toward excellent solutions as quickly and cheaply as possible, e.g., in terms of overall duration and participant effort.

- *Good documentation*: We should clearly document the outputs of the deliberation in a way that makes it quick and easy to find what we need to know, e.g., which solutions were proposed for what challenges, as well as what their strengths and weaknesses are. This is important both to support the deliberation process as well as to support those in the future who wish to understand and learn from the decisions that we made.

How well do existing technologies fare? In the following, we will enumerate the barriers that these tools face in terms of enabling effective deliberation at scale. While this analysis is no doubt incomplete, it has been informed by analyzing many deliberation engagements described in the literature as well as by decades of experience with running face-to-face and computer-supported deliberation engagements with a wide range of topics and customers and with groups ranging from small teams to crowds of several hundred participants. Our list includes the most serious and common challenges we encountered. The barriers, organized by the goal that they impact, include:

3.2 Goal: Excellent ideation

3.2.1 Barrier: Shallow answers

Online crowd deliberations tend to generate large numbers of relatively shallow answers that come from individual users, rather than a smaller number of more deeply considered, collaboratively developed answers. In other words, while we do benefit from casting a wide net for ideas, we do not elicit a lot of idea synergy. This represents a lost opportunity for getting superior solutions from the crowd. One important reason for this, we believe, is that collaborative idea development is not well supported in conversation-centric platforms.

3.2.2 Barrier: Crypto-content

We have observed that many of the answers and arguments contributed in online deliberations can be terse and idiomatic. The authors essentially trust that the other participants will share enough context with the author to understand their posts. This can however lead to what we call "crypto-posts," especially when the crowd is diverse and, as a result, many participants do not share context in that way.

3.3 Goal: Comprehensive critiquing

3.3.1 Barrier: Argument paucity

Online deliberations tend to produce a relatively small number of arguments per answer. In our last 14 online deliberation engagements, for example, each including between 20 and 150 participants, answers got just a few arguments each. The arguments are also often lacking in terms of logical rigor and supporting evidence. The "many eyes" effect, in other word, is under-utilized, with the likely result that important strengths (and perhaps more importantly, *weaknesses*) of candidate answers aren't identified.

3.4 Goal: Accurate filtering

3.4.1 Barrier: Rating paucity

It can be difficult to get a lot of ratings on answers in online deliberations. In our last two large-scale deliberation engagements for example, both involving about 100 participants each, we got an average of about 10 ratings per answer. This represents, in our judgment, the most serious impediment to effective scalable deliberations, because it means that they will all-too-often just create large piles of answers with no clear winners.

Why does this happen? Online deliberations create an "embarrassment of riches" [13]. Even relatively small crowds, when addressing complex topics, can quickly produce large answer sets, simply because complex challenges inherently have many potential solutions, and people are creative at finding them. In one of our recent online deliberation engagements, for example, a crowd of about 100 people generated a corpus of over 600 answers in about 2 hours. To get just 10 ratings per answer, with two selection criteria, each crowd member had to do 120 ratings. The rating burden is exacerbated by the fact that participants are asked to carefully review the arguments associated with each answer before submitting their ratings (so they can benefit from the many eyes effect) and rating often comes at the end of a long deliberation, when participants are tired. Rating is also less fun, less creative, than ideating and arguing. All this makes it a lot to ask. But a paucity of rating means that the "wisdom of crowds" effect is under-utilized: we end up with a lot of answers but only a rudimentary idea of which ones truly belong at the top.

3.5 Goal: Good documentation

3.5.1 Barrier: Disorganized content

A well-documented deliberation is one where it is easy for participants to find the content they want. It should be easy, for example, to find all the proposed answers to a given question, or all the arguments for and against a given answer. But this is almost never the case in online deliberations: the content is essentially a pile of comments organized by the time they were contributed and/or the other comments they responded to. The answers for a given question, or the arguments for a given answer, may be spread arbitrarily throughout the corpus. Content that is not readily accessible is effectively lost: many potentially valuable insights may be lost in the pile.

3.6 Goal: Maximal efficiency

3.6.1 Barrier: Haphazard effort allocation

When you have a deliberation of even moderate size, a critical concern becomes making sure that the crowd members devote their time to the tasks *where they can do the most good*, i.e., to the tasks that they are most qualified to perform and that are most likely to lead to pareto-optimal solutions. In our most recent deliberation, for example, about 100 people generated 600 answers, which all potentially need to be commented on, critiqued, and rated. A participant in this deliberation would thus have *1800* choices for which action to take next. How can they choose well? Current deliberation tools do little or nothing to address this critical need. People tend to flock to the most recently-contributed content and/or the content that has received the most attention, often because it is highly controversial. None of that ensures that the crowd progresses efficiently toward excellent solutions.

3.6.2 Barrier: Noise

Deliberations can sometimes be plagued by low signal-to-noise ratios, caused by a surfeit of redundant, toxic, or simply vacuous content[2] [13–15]. This is highly dependent, however, on the nature of the crowd and the topic and the discussion medium. We've found, for example, that deliberations hosted on structured deliberation mapping platforms have substantially less toxicity than those hosted on unstructured conversation platforms [15].

3.7 Goal: Correct selection

3.7.1 Barrier: Tradeoff opacity

Even if the answers, arguments, and ratings contributed by a crowd are organized systematically using something like a deliberation map, the decision-makers for the deliberation still face substantial challenges. It is straightforward to present them with

[2] This includes, for example, arguments that simply say "good idea" without giving a reason. In one recent deliberation engagement, for example, over 25% of the arguments were vacuous in this way.

	Feasible	Effective
Professors must supervise only in their area of specialization	4.9	3.8
Create a listening unit for researchers	4.0	4.8
PhD students should assume responsibility early	3.8	4.9

Figure 2.
An example of a deliberation summary report.

a summary of the answers and the ratings they got for the assessment criteria, for example as we do it in the Deliberatorium (**Figure 2**).

There are however tradeoffs to be made concerning how well the answers satisfy the different criteria. This information is available in the summary above but not in a way that makes the tradeoffs quick and easy to understand. There are also tradeoffs to be made concerning the impact on the different stakeholder groups. Most answers will benefit stakeholders unevenly, and understanding this is important because, if the benefits of the selected answers are too unbalanced, this can lead to potentially fatal resistance against their implementation. How can decision-makers wrest the insights they need from deliberations that may involve hundreds of answers and arguments, hundreds of participants, and thousands of ratings?

4. How AI can help

The recent stunning advances in AI, particularly in large language models, seem to represent an epochal advance in how well computers can understand and engage in human discourse. How can we harness this to enable better deliberation at scale? In this section, we will describe the emerging solutions that our group has been exploring for each of the barriers identified above.

4.1 Barrier: Disorganized content

A basic requirement of effective large-scale deliberation is to make it as easy as possible for interested parties (such as decision makers as well as people who want to learn from past deliberations) to find what has been said on any particular topic. But, as we have seen, conventional conversation-centric approaches to deliberation create large and disorganized "comment piles" where valuable ideas can easily be lost.

In our own work, we have used a technique called "deliberation mapping" to organize user contributions to a deliberation. Instead of people freely adding comments wherever and however they want, they are asked to collaboratively create a simple but powerful knowledge schema called a "deliberation map" [16]. A map is a tree structure consisting of *questions* to be answered, *criteria* that describe the attributes of good answers, possible *answers* for the questions, pro and con *arguments* that support or rebut an idea in the map, and *ratings* that capture how well the answers satisfy the assessment criteria. Answers can raise questions, and arguments can support/rebut other arguments, so a map consists of a core of interleaved questions and answers plus "halos" of pros and cons around the answers. For example (**Figure 3**).

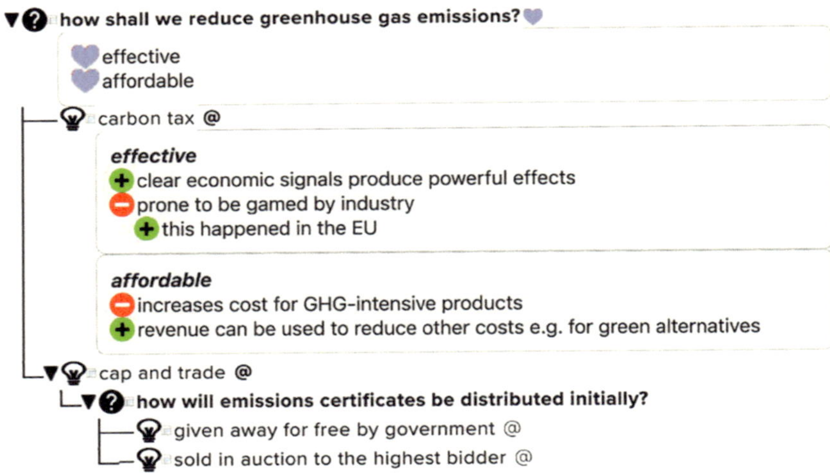

Figure 3.
An example of a deliberation map.

In this map, the question is: "how can we reduce greenhouse gas emissions?." The criteria for a *good* answer are that it be *effective* and *affordable*. Two candidate answers were proposed: "carbon tax" and "cap and trade," each with their own pros and cons. Someone has raised a question, further, about how the answer "cap and trade" should be implemented.

Deliberation maps have important advantages over conversation-centric deliberations. All the points appear in the part of the map they logically belong: all answers to a question are attached to that question in the map, and all arguments are attached to the answer they concern. It is therefore easy to find all the crowd's input on any given topic. *Gaps* in the deliberation—e.g., questions without any answers, or answers without any arguments—are also easy to identify, so we can guide crowd members to fill in these gaps and foster more complete coverage. All competing ideas and arguments are right next to each other, negating the possible ill effects of clique formation and undercutting the perverse incentives that lead to extremization and toxicity. Making arguments into first-class entities implicitly encourages participants to express the evidence and logic for/against competing answers [17]. Users, finally, can easily collaborate to refine proposed solutions. One user can, for example, propose an answer, a second raise a question about how that answer can achieve a given requirement, and a third propose possible answers for that sub-question. Deliberation maps can be applied to a comprehensive range of deliberation types, ranging from simple question answering to design, diagnosis, prediction and planning tasks, while remaining simple to use and easy to understand [18].

The author's team has developed a crowd-scale deliberation mapping platform called the "Deliberatorium" [19] and conducted multiple evaluations of how well it helps real-world organizations (e.g., BP, Intel, the University of Naples, the Federal Bureau of Land Management, the Italian Democratic Party, UM6P University, and OCP) deliberate on complex topics (e.g., bio-fuels use, oil platform maintenance, water use rights, climate change solutions, electoral law reform, university research, and fertilizer manufacture). These engagements have included as many as 400 participants and generated maps with as many as 1600 answers and arguments.

In our observations of these deliberation engagements, we have noted that roughly 20% of the answers and arguments that people contribute have structural issues such as:

- *Misplaced* (e.g., an answer is attached to the wrong question)
- *Mistyped* (e.g., someone puts an answer into a PRO argument, or puts an argument in an answer)
- *Bundled* (e.g., a persons' answer includes *several* answers and arguments in a single post). We've encountered posts with as many as 10 distinct points.

These are problematic since it means that the content is in effect misfiled—it's not collocated with the other content on that topic—and therefore effectively *lost*. Bundling is especially pernicious because it means that *all* the points in the post may thereby be misfiled. Bundling also undercuts our ability to critique and rate people's ideas. If an answer has several ideas in it, how do we critique and rate it? We might like one of the ideas and dislike others, but we have no direct way to indicate which is which.

In previous work we used human moderators to check submitted posts for such problems and, through a dialog with the author, correct them, before the posts were published to the map for all to see. While this is workable, developing software that can eliminate or at least greatly reduce the amount of human moderation effort clearly is advantageous in terms of reducing the costs of running a deliberation as well as reducing the time it takes before a users' post is published to the map where others can benefit from it. How can we do this?

4.1.1 Solution: The unbundler

Our team has been developing the "unbundler" tool to meet this challenge. It uses LLMs to take the posts contributed by users, break them into their constituent points, give these points the correct type (answer, pro, or con) and identify where these points should be placed in the map. For example, here is what the unbundler did on a recent deliberation engagement:

Context

Question: How can we improve on our master's degree curriculum?

Original post

Some say there is too much homework. Some say homework is good. Some weeks are homework-free while some weeks are homework-overwhelming. If only there is a way professors can coordinate to distribute workloads across the semester.

Unbundler output

```
[
        []      "type": "barrier",
                "text": "There is too much homework assigned in the SCI
                master's program.",
                "children": [
                []          "type": "con",
                  "text": "Homework is good."
                }
        ]
    },
```

[] "type": "barrier",
"text": "The distribution of homework varies significantly, with some weeks being homework-free and others being overwhelming."
},
[] "type": "solution",
"text": "Professors should coordinate to better distribute homework workloads across the semester."
}
]

In our earlier work, reported in [20], we achieved an unbundling accuracy of roughly 70%. Our more recent work, which has benefited from better prompt engineering as well as improved LLMs, is now roughly 90% accurate, which we consider high enough to put in front of users in real-world engagements. In these engagements, the unbundler will suggest how to unbundle content, but the authors will be able to review and correct any mistakes made by the unbundler before the re-structured post is entered into the map.

4.2 Barrier: Crypto-content

We've observed than a substantial fraction of the posts in our Deliberatorium engagements are what we called "crypto-content," i.e., posts that by virtue of terse descriptions or specialized vocabulary were hard for many of the other deliberation participants to understand. This was especially an issue in deliberations where the participants were linguistically diverse and often had to interact in other than their native language. In the Deliberatorium, users are asked to provide a short title for their answer in addition to a more detailed description. We noted that the titles were especially prone to being cryptic.

4.2.1 Solution: Content re-statement

Our group has been exploring whether LLMs can address this issue. We provide the LLM with the users' post as well as the *context* for that post, e.g., if the LLM is re-stating an answer, we provide the question that answer was responding to. We then ask the LLM to re-state the post. The user can accept the re-statement as is, modify it to correct any errors, or add additional text to their post and ask the LLM to try re-stating it again.

Here's an example from an engagement we conducted recently with a university:

Context

Question: How can we achieve success in research?

Answer: Involve PhD students in decision-making, enhance recognition of contributions.

Original post

PRO: they are the most concerns, it is a real-time foster.

LLM output

PhD students are the most directly affected by research-related decisions, and involving them can help foster a more responsive and supportive research environment in real time.

Our preliminary evaluations show that LLMs do a remarkably good job of clearly re-stating most posts, with the added benefit of converting them into clear uniform and non-toxic[3] language. This means that ideas are more likely to be judged based on their merits rather than on idiosyncrasies of their wording. We also noted that, generally, if the LLM re-states the content incorrectly, it probably would have been difficult for a human to understand and it was thus probably important for the user to clarify. The LLM thus adds value even, or perhaps especially, when it initially fails to capture the users' intent.

4.3 Barrier: Shallow answers

As we noted above, online deliberations tend to create lots of relatively shallow single-user contributions. The answers are not very detailed and rarely benefit from the "idea synergy" you get when multiple people work together to develop an idea.

One possibility solution is to simply directly ask LLMs to suggest answers to the deliberation questions. This is straightforward to implement and, in our experience, can reliably generate large numbers of relevant contributions. There are however two key challenges to this approach: the *specificity* and *creativity* gaps.

The specificity gap: LLMs tend to generate highly *generic* content. They in effect regurgitate, as an inherent result of how they are developed, the most frequently-appearing answers from their training sets. This has a number of disadvantages. One of course is that the best answer for a given context may not be one of the more common ones in the training set. It may be accessible if you give a very specific prompt, but it's unclear of course what that prompt would be. There is also the issue of coverage. It has been estimated that only about 10% of the data on the internet is public and thus available for inclusion in LLM training sets. Much of this data comes from a relatively small portion of the globe's population, developed Western countries with widespread use of digital media. Let us say for example I work for a fertilizer company in Morocco. How much is an LLM going to know about the specific challenges constraints and resources my company has?

Add to this that an enormous amount of human knowledge has not been captured in the textual form needed to train LLMs. Few people put all their useful knowledge in written form, especially if they consider it "common sense" that everyone should already know. And there are vast swaths of valuable "tacit" human knowledge, such as physical skills, honed intuitions, and so on, that are probably not adequately captured as text. All this implies that the best answers for problems with specialized circumstances may either be difficult to access or simply not available in the model. After all, even the largest LLMs currently take up less than a terabyte of disk space, which can be stored in a drive the size of a pack of playing cards. No compression algorithm is able to distill all human knowledge into such tight quarters.

While extraordinary in many ways, LLMs in their current state are thus *unlikely* to produce answers that are deeply specific to the circumstances of the requestor.

The creativity gap: LLMs, as we noted above, inherently regurgitate (with some generalization) what humans have said in the past. While this can be enormously valuable, humans can create *new* ideas, in a process that still remains largely mysterious but which seems to build upon human diversity as well as our ability to combine diverse ideas to create something quite new.

[3] Interestingly, the use of toxic language in deliberations is deeply influenced by the kind of tool people use to deliberate. Our research has shown that conventional conversation-centric deliberations have much higher toxicity levels than structured conversations based, for example, on deliberation mapping [15].

Consider this simple thought experiment [21]. Let us say that human beings have, in aggregate, a total of 100 unique cognitive skills[4]: math, drawing, mental rotation, empathy, complex movement, musical performance, and so on. Let us say that each individual has 50 of those skills, randomly selected from this skill pool. How many unique skill combinations ("cognitive types") of humans are there? This is a simple combinatorial math problem:

$$\binom{100}{50} = \frac{100!}{50! \cdot (100-50)!} \approx 1.0089 \times 10^{29} \tag{1}$$

There are *100 octillion* possible combinations. Every human being who ever lived, or who will ever exist for that matter, is thus very likely to be cognitively unique and potentially capable of creating unique solutions, since we are each doing so based on unique collections of building blocks. It is possible, even likely, that we each have some particular problem(s) that we can solve better than anyone else. That is why "casting a wide net" can be so powerful. We can take this even further. It has been widely observed that new ideas often come from "idea synergy," i.e., from combining the diverse ideas that come from diverse individuals. Since every individual is unique, every collaboration represents an unprecedented combination with the potential for creative synergies that have never been explored before. LLMs, however, come from largely the same training sets (the publicly available internet) so the diversity across LLMs is relatively low. And there is still little evidence that LLMs can generate, on their own, truly novel ideas, as opposed to simply novel combinations of existing ones. LLMs are thus unlikely to result to create genuinely new ideas.

While LLM-generated answers can represent a useful starting point for solving problems, the specificity and creativity gaps imply that they will need significant human involvement. We have explored several different approaches to addressing this problem, inspired by how people assist each other when brainstorming.

4.3.1 Solution: Pregnant questions

One way we can support each other's ideation is through what we can call "pregnant questions." Let us say for example that I am searching for solutions to the problem of ethics violations in research. My initial idea is to implement a system of rewards for exemplary ethical research behavior. A colleague who is trying to help might then ask me something like "what criteria will you use to define exemplary ethical research behavior?." Answering that question leads me to deepen my answer. We can extend that process over multiple iterations, where each answer gets its own pregnant questions, resulting eventually in a highly detailed answer. Even if we know less about the specifics of a problem than the person we are trying to help, it is still in our observation often possible for us to ask useful pregnant questions.

We have implemented a version of this concept, which we call the "deep dive ideator." In it, the LLM suggests questions intended to help a user refine his/her answer, in addition to, on request, suggesting "starter answers" for the user to build upon (**Figure 4**).

[4] This is probably a highly conservative estimate, since we are only considering the diversity that results from skill differences. A truer accounting would also consider, for example, how people differ in knowledge and experiences.

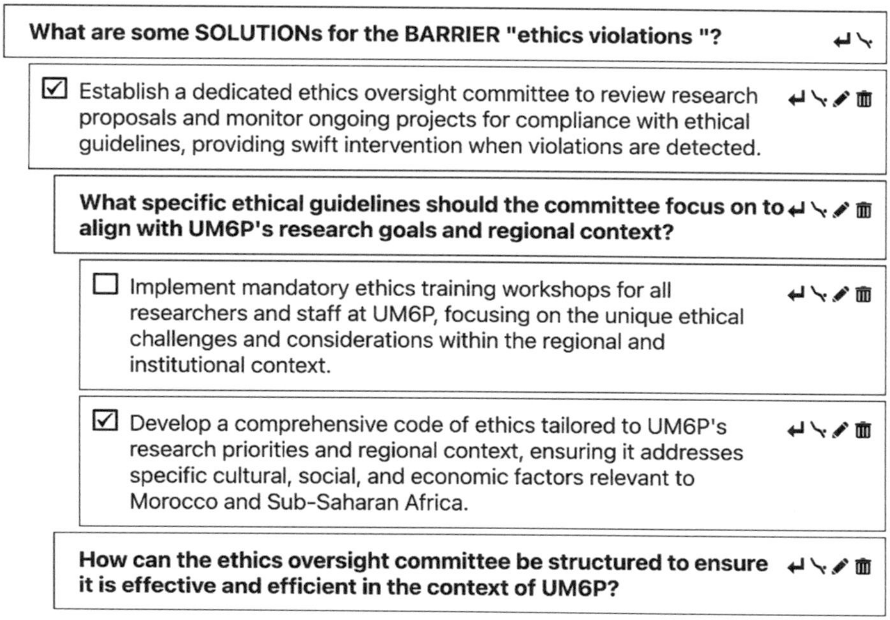

Figure 4.
A snapshot of the deep dive ideator. The LLM-generated questions are **bold.**

Our observation to date is that LLMs can do an excellent job of proposing useful pregnant questions and starter answers. Even if we just select from among the LLM-proposed questions and answers, rather than proposing any of our own, we can create a substantially localized answer, because we'll pick the questions and answers that seem most useful for our particular context. We can thus use the collaboration of LLMs and humans to ameliorate the specificity gap that LLMs face while still taking advantage of their unprecedented breadth of building-block ideas.

4.3.2 Solution: Creativity cues

Another tack we have begun to pursue is using LLMs to *cue* human creativity, rather than attempt to replace it. Research on human creativity has found that people tend to generate more creative ideas when inspired by unusual/unlikely cues, such as:

- Unusual *combinations* of other ideas (e.g., "Describe a startup idea that combines farming and blockchain")

- Unusual *constraints* on the solutions (e.g., "Invent a board game that could be played on Mars using only stones and string.")

Work on LLM-assisted creativity has begun to explore how these creativity cues can be generated by LLMs rather than by other people [22–24].

Our work, since it is specifically aimed at improving ideation in the context of scalable multi-criteria decision-making, is exploring the idea of cueing people with combinations of ideas that are semantically diverse (as above) but also *complimentary* in their strengths and weaknesses. Imagine that deliberation participants have

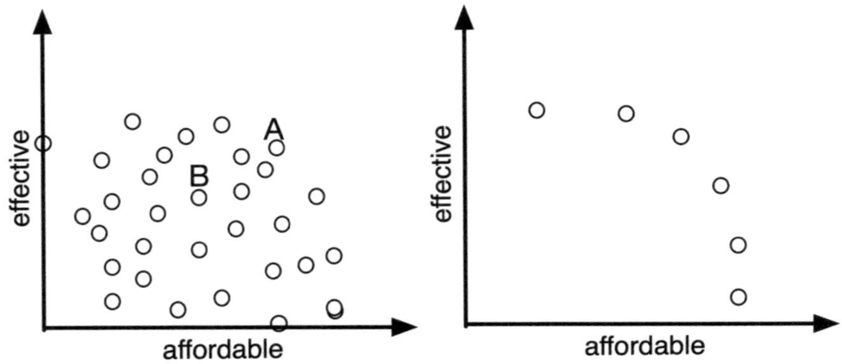

Figure 5.
An example of a utility diagram and its pareto-optimal front.

developed a set of answers and rated them with respect to the assessment criteria. We can capture this information using a utility diagram (**Figure 5**).

The figure on the left is the utility diagram. Each circle in that diagram represents a candidate answer. Its location corresponds to the scores it got from the crowd for how well it satisfies the assessment criteria (in this case, how *affordable* and *effective* the answer is). Note that in some cases one answer can *dominate* another, i.e., it can be equal or better than the other with respect to *all* the assessment criteria. Answer A above, for example, dominates answer B. If we remove all the dominated answers from the utility diagram, we end up with the pareto-optimal front, shown on the right. As we noted in Section 3, finding the pareto front is a basic requirement for a successful deliberation. If we fail to do so, we risk missing solutions that are better *from every perspective* than what we have considered so far. Building from this concept, our idea is to present users with creativity cues consisting of two or more answers that are (as with other efforts) semantically diverse[5] but that also come from *opposite ends of the pareto front.* These answers will have, by definition, *complementary* strengths and weaknesses, and the hope is that the user will be inspired to invent new answers that combine those strengths.

4.3.3 Solution: Contextualization

Another approach to ameliorating the specificity gap is to ask LLMs to specify *what context information they need* to provide the best possible answers. We call this the "contextualization" tool. Here's an example:

Input to LLM

I work for a large research university. My goal is to maintain the reputation of the university by minimizing research ethics violations. I need help finding solutions that will work in my specific context. I want you to tell me what you need to know about my context in order to provide me with good solutions. Please frame what you need to know in the form of questions for me to answer.

LLM-generated questions

---

[5] We use an LLM, in this case, to *assess* which combinations of answers are the most diverse and therefore the most potentially generative.

What office or department is responsible for overseeing research ethics (e.g., Office of Research Integrity, IRB, Compliance Office)?

What is your role, and what level of authority do you have over policies, enforcement, or training?

What are the major research disciplines represented at your university (e.g., biomedical, social sciences, engineering, humanities)?

Are there particular areas where violations are more likely or have occurred more frequently (e.g., human subjects research, data fabrication, authorship disputes)?

<*These are 3 of the 18 questions suggested by the LLM*>

Once the human user has answered the contextualization questions, these responses are provided as background to help ensure that subsequent LLM outputs are more focused on the users' context. This will however probably be a resource-intensive endeavor. In the example above, the LLM asked *18* questions to provide context for addressing just one user goal. It may only make sense to do if this cost is amortized over many related deliberation questions.

4.4 Barrier: Argument paucity

As noted above, online deliberations tend to produce a relatively small number of arguments per answer, and the arguments are frequently non-rigorous. This deeply undercuts our ability to filter and select answers accurately.

It is of course possible to ask LLMs to suggest critiques for candidate answers [25–27]. But should we do so, we are likely to again hit the specificity gap. The pros and cons for an answer are, of course, often deeply dependent on the specific *context* in which it will be implemented. But unless we have comprehensively fine-tuned an LLM specifically for our context, which few have the resources to do, we can expect the LLM to just generate the generic pros and cons that appeared most commonly in the training set. There's a risk that, without human intervention, irrelevant or even misleading arguments will be proposed and important ones neglected. But human contributions are often of mixed quality. What can we do about this?

4.4.1 Solution: The argument structure advisor

One solution we are working on is an LLM-based "argument structure advisor," which applies the same kind of diagnose-and-repair process that a helpful human colleague might follow. It is based on the observation that we can help someone improve their arguments, even if we are not a deep expert in their domain, by checking for problems with the *structure* of the arguments. Examples of such structural problems include unstated assumptions, lack of evidence, logical fallacies, cognitive biases, appeal to emotion, and so on. Since the approach focuses on structural rather than context-specific issues, it can *avoid the specificity gap*.

We start by presenting the LLM with the argument to review, along with its context (i.e., which answer the argument addressed, what question that answer is responding to). For example:

Context
Question: how can we measure success in research at our university?
Answer: measure the level of research funding that our university receives.
Argument
Con: funding could potentially degrade research quality.

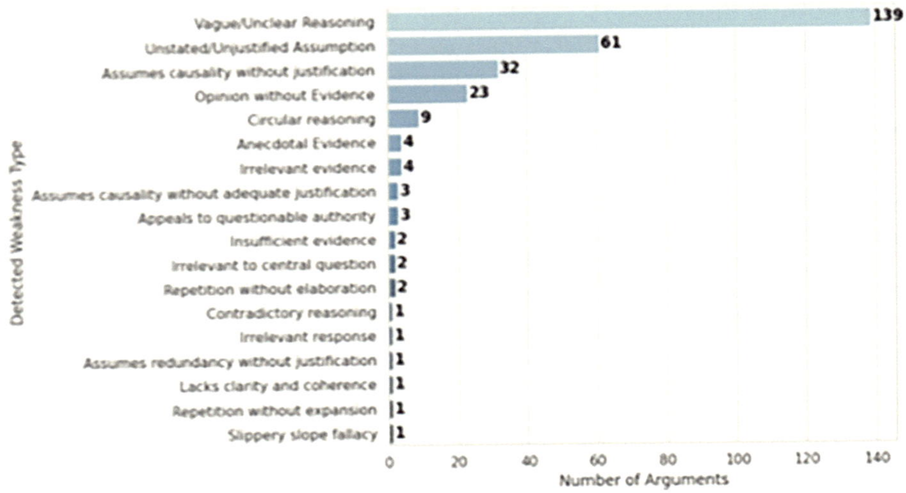

Figure 6.
Distribution of LLM-detected weaknesses in an argument corpus.

The LLM is asked to identify potential structural weaknesses with the argument. When applied to the argument above, for example, an LLM identified an unstated assumption:

> The argument assumes that increased funding will degrade research quality without providing evidence or reasoning to support this claim.

When we applied this prompt to a collection of ~300 arguments generated in a recent deliberation engagement, we found the following distribution of argument weakness types (**Figure 6**).

An LLM is next asked to offer advice on how to repair the identified weakness with the argument. For the example above, for instance, the argument advisor suggested the following:

> Clarify how funding could negatively impact research.

We assessed this approach using the argument quality scoring tool described in [28], which provides the following quality measures:

- *Clarity*: Whether the argument is clear, concise, and easily understandable.
- *Structure*: Whether the argument structure contributes to the presentation of the viewpoints.
- *Relevance*: Whether the argument directly addresses the debate issue.

We applied the argument structure advisor to about 300 pro and con arguments retrieved from a human deliberation about improving research quality in a university.

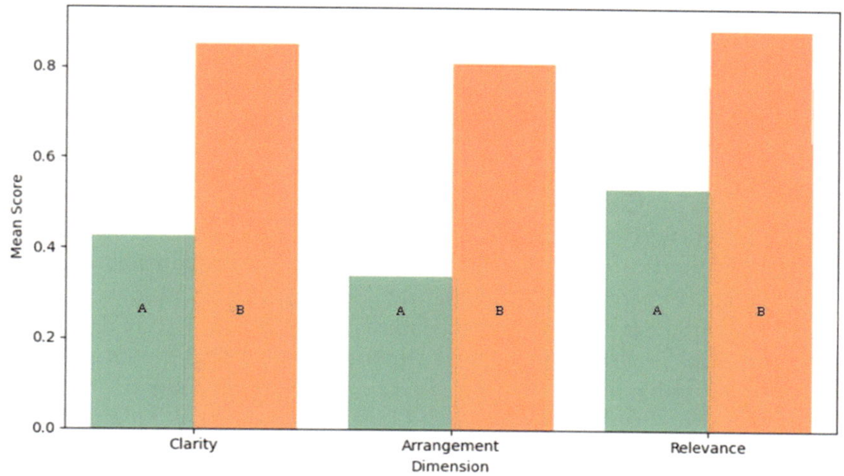

Figure 7.
Impact of argument advisor on argument quality scores. Version A is the argument before the advisor, version B is after.

The advisor identified structural weaknesses and suggested what the user could do to address them. We then—in the interest of rapid testing—used an LLM to update the argument based on that suggestion, rather than asking the human author of the original argument to do so.

The following bar chart summarizes the argument quality scores before and after application of the argument structure advisor. The scores run from 0 (poor) to 1 (excellent) (**Figure 7**).

As we can see, the argument quality scores roughly doubled after applying the argument advisor. The differences between the before-after quality scores were all statistically significant with a p-value of $\sim 10^{-50}$.

In these initial proof-of-concept tests, the argument advisor updated the users' arguments post-hoc, without their participation. It is therefore of course possible that our tool misinterpreted the users' intent. We are now developing an *interactive* version of the argument advisor, which identifies possible weaknesses in the user's argument and suggests possible fixes, but where the user makes/selects the changes that best reflect what they intended to say.

4.4.2 Solution: Lemon agents

There is a fundamental epistemic asymmetry involved in critiquing ideas. It's generally much easier to identify the *weaknesses* of an idea than its *strengths* [29]. You can often identify bad ideas based on a single failed assumption, using just common sense or general knowledge. But authoritatively identifying good ideas generally means systematically *rebutting* all the possible weaknesses first, which can require a huge amount of specialized expertise. One way, therefore, to avoid the specificity gap in critiquing is to focus the LLM on identifying cons (i.e., finding "lemons") rather than pros. We can rely on human experts and stakeholders to provide the specialized expertise needed to identify more localized cons as well as reliable pro arguments. Our "lemon agent" project is exploring that concept, initially in the realm of medical diagnosis.

4.5 Barrier: Rating paucity

As noted above, even moderate-scale deliberation engagements tend to produce a *lot* of answers, creating a potentially prohibitive rating burden for the deliberation participants and as a result a paucity of ratings per answer. In the absence of effective filtering, however, all the crowd has created is a giant answer pile with no clear winners.

One possibility is to offload rating from human participants altogether, instructing LLMs to rate answers with respect to the relevant criteria, taking into account the arguments contributed for those answers. But this faces the specificity gap in an especially pernicious way. There is simply too much tacit and localized human knowledge involved in making such judgments. Assessment is the most *context-specific* part of deliberation, requiring knowledge—e.g., of the customer's resources, leadership, culture, and history—that LLMs probably will not have. It is in addition notoriously difficult to formally capture people's utility functions for assessing complex ideas, since so much of it is difficult to verbalize. This leads to a high risk that the LLM ratings will miss important concerns as well as over-emphasize unimportant ones. What can we do about this?

4.5.1 Solution: Answer clustering

Our current approach to this challenge is to find ways that LLMs can help humans assess answers more quickly, rather than replacing humans altogether. Our answer-clustering project, more specifically, uses LLMs to "compress" an answer corpus into clusters whose members have shared strengths and weaknesses. We then ask the crowd to assess (critique and rate) compact summaries of these clusters and thereby eliminate the low-rated clusters from further consideration. Only answers from the *highest-rated* clusters then need be individually assessed. In more detail, we:

- Use an LLM to *augment* the answers by adding pro and con arguments to them. This is the key trick: it helps ensure that we cluster together answers that share similar strengths and weaknesses.
- Use an LLM[6] to *cluster* these augmented answers. Since the primary goal of our approach is to quickly eliminate answer clusters that do not merit further attention, the LLM is instructed to pay particular attention to clustering together answers that have shared weaknesses.
- Use an LLM to generate a *summary* of the answers in each cluster.
- Ask the crowd to *assess* (critique and rate) these cluster summaries.
- Identify the *best* clusters, i.e., those that are on (or near) the pareto-dominant front.
- Ask the crowd to assess the *individual* answers only in the pareto-dominant clusters.

[6] We found that LLM-generated clusters had significantly higher cluster quality scores, in our context, than the more conventional approach of applying K-Means to the text embeddings for the augmented answer descriptions.

This approach potentially saves a lot of time and effort. Imagine for example that we have an answer corpus of 400 ideas (which in our experience is a typical size for a brainstorming engagement of 100 people working for an hour). Let us say we use an LLM to find 20 clusters of 20 answers each, and 20% (i.e., 4) of these clusters are on or near the pareto front (also typical in our experience). In this example, the crowd will have been asked to assess 100 answer descriptions (20 cluster summaries plus 4 * 20 answers) rather than 400—a fourfold speedup in the assessment process. If the answer corpus is large enough to warrant it, we can speed up the assessment further by applying this process *recursively*, i.e., we can use the cluster-rating mechanism to speed up the assessment of the answers *within* large clusters.

The key question of course is whether we can create clusters whose answers share enough strengths and weaknesses that they can safely be eliminated at the cluster level. If we do this poorly, we risk eliminating clusters that have some superior ideas in them. This risk is unavoidable, of course, if we do not have the resources to evaluate every individual answer in depth, but we do want to minimize it. Cluster quality has accordingly been the KPI for our project, measured as follows:

- For each cluster, we use an LLM to generate "cluster arguments," i.e., a set of pros and cons based on reviewing the cluster description.
- We use an LLM to score *how well* these arguments apply to the cluster members. An ideal cluster is one in which the cluster arguments fully apply to all the answers within the cluster.

Our manual spot-checking suggests that this metric does an adequate job of assessing cluster quality, and it has the great advantage of being much faster and cheaper than hiring humans to code how well the cluster arguments apply to the member answers.

Using this metric, we evaluated our answer clustering code with 134 answers generated by a recent deliberation on how a major research university could increase its research productivity. Here is one of the 20 clusters generated, by the clustering tool, for these answers (**Table 1**).

Our current approach achieves an average cluster quality score of 6.3/7 over our test set of 134 answers, which seems quite promising. We have yet to experimentally confirm however whether these clusters indeed increase assessment speed without sacrificing accuracy in real-world deliberation engagements with human participants.

4.6 Barrier: Noise

As noted above, deliberations can sometimes be plagued by low signal-to-noise ratios, caused by a surfeit of redundant, toxic, or simply vacuous content.

4.6.1 Solution: Semantic filtering

Our initial tests suggest that LLMs are imperfect but still very useful at substantially reducing the level of noise in scalable deliberations by identifying posts that are redundant, toxic, or vacuous, using a combination of text embeddings and prompt

Title	Leveraging collaboration
Summary	This cluster centers on using collaboration—across disciplines, institutions, sectors, and regions—as a primary mechanism for enhancing research success. The answers emphasize that collaborative efforts can drive innovation, broaden resource access, and increase research impact, while also serving as tangible indicators (e.g., joint publications, partnerships, or platform activity) for institutional performance. Common logical approaches include prioritizing measurable outputs from partnerships, fostering interdisciplinary or cross-sectoral teams, and institutionalizing collaboration through policy or funding.
Answers in cluster	• Collaborate across sectors: industry, government, NGOs • Build strong partnerships with universities, research institutions, and industry partners • Joint African university research programs • Foster interdisciplinary collaboration for complex problem-solving • Work together with peers • Establish open digital platform for collaborative research requests • Foster collaboration with African entities for joint research success • Partner with university labs • Enhance interdisciplinary cross-departmental collaboration • Qualities of being a successful researcher: curiosity, collaboration, and thorough literature exploration • Knowledge sharing • Allocate funding for fostering internal collaborations
LLM-generated arguments	• PRO: Collaboration enables access to diverse expertise and resources, allowing for more ambitious and innovative research projects. • PRO: Joint efforts enhance institutional reputation, attract funding, and provide measurable outputs (such as co-authored publications or partnership agreements). • PRO: Collaborative structures can address complex, real-world problems more effectively than isolated research efforts. • CON: Coordination across partners, disciplines, or sectors can be administratively burdensome and slow down research progress. • CON: Measuring the true impact or attributing success within collaborations is often complex, potentially diluting recognition or skewing assessment. • CON: There is a risk of superficial or forced partnerships that prioritize quantity over quality, as well as possible conflicts of interest or loss of institutional identity.
Cluster quality	6.16/7

Table 1.
An example of an answer cluster.

engineering. This is being used, in the Deliberatorium (our deliberation platform) to encourage participants to improve their posts as they are creating them, as well as to tag problematic posts for attention by a human moderator if necessary post-hoc. Again, there is a division of labor: the LLMs are used to suggest possible problems but the final judgments are made by human post authors or moderators.

4.7 Barrier: Haphazard effort allocation

When you have a large corpus of potential answers and arguments, a critical component of ensuring an efficient deliberation is making sure that the crowd members devote their time to the tasks *where they can do the most good*. We call this "attention mediation." Our earlier work relied solely on easy-to-calculate "map gap" scores to matchmake users with the map posts that have received the least amount of attention so far. An answer that has not been critiqued by many people, for example, will have a higher priority than one which has had many critiques. This helps ensure that no posts are lost in the crowd. But this is only part of the solution, since it neither takes into account individual differences in what different users can/want to do, nor does it focus effort on the answers that are most likely to be pareto optimal. We are exploring several approaches to addressing these gaps.

4.7.1 Solution: User model agents

One potentially powerful way to address the attention mediation challenge is to develop accurate models of each participants' knowledge, skills and interests, ideally just by observing what they do in deliberations (and how other people react to it). We can use these user models, in conjunction with the "map gap" scores, to identify the best deliberation actions for a user to do next.

Existing techniques for making such recommendations (e.g., for which movies to see or books to purchase) rely mainly on collaborative filtering, i.e., on seeing what choices were popular with people who are statistically similar to you. This requires acquiring a large corpus of data on what choices people have made in the past, but this is problematic in a deliberation context because the set of choices (i.e., the set of posts that a person could attend to) are open-ended and constantly growing as the deliberation proceeds. We need a way to assess whether newly added deliberation posts are *semantically similar* to those that the user (or people like him/her) have successfully contributed to in the past.

Our concept is to use LLMs to make these kinds of semantic inferences by creating user model agents for each participant. These agents will be fed a stream of data about what suggested actions the user has elected *not* to do in the past, what the user *has* chosen to do (in terms of adding answers, arguments, ratings), as well as how these contributions have been *responded* to by the crowd. We can then ask the user model agents to infer what new answers the user will most willing and able to address effectively. Our hypothesis is that LLM-based user model agents will be able to use the vast amount of background knowledge they incorporate to do this effectively with much less historical data than is required by conventional, purely statistical, approaches. Our KPIs for this work will include reducing the number of suggestions that the user rejects, as well as increasing the average rating given by the crowd to what the users do contribute.

4.7.2 Solution: Assessment optimization

As we noted above, getting enough answer ratings in collective deliberations is a serious issue. One way to mitigate this problem is to be smarter in terms of *which* answers we ask the crowd to rate. The goal of a deliberation, remember, is to find the answers on the pareto-optimal front. Once an answer is statistically very unlikely to join the pareto front, there is no point in asking for further ratings for that answer. We are exploring the use of Monte Carlo simulations to determine which ratings have the highest value in terms of identifying which posts belong on the pareto front [30].

4.7.3 Solution: Answer search optimization

Answer generation in complex domains inherently creates combinatoric explosions. This is because a complete answer will typically involve coming up with answers to a set of *interdependent sub-questions*, i.e., where the best answer to one question depends on the choices that have been made for the *other* questions [30, 31]. Imagine for example that we are deliberating about the design for a car. We have to decide about the passenger layout, storage layout, the power train, the engine, and so on. These decisions are all inter-dependent, since for example the right power train choice depends on which engine we choose. If we have just 10 interdependent questions to answer, and just 10 alternatives per question, this creates a space of 10^{10} (10 billion) possible alternatives for the car design. This is clearly too large for any crowd to explore exhaustively, so we have to make smart choices about how to search it.

This is in essence a nonlinear optimization problem and many techniques, such as tabu search, simulated annealing, and genetic algorithms, have been developed to address it. But these techniques make assumptions that are typically not satisfied in scalable deliberation. For example, they generally assume that a reasonably accurate utility function (which maps a proposed answer to a numeric estimate of how good it is) is readily available, quick, and cheap to run, so many alternatives can be assessed in short order. When the utility function is actually the aggregate result of many humans rating answers, these assumptions do not hold: assessing answer utility is expensive and slow and the results have variable accuracy.

This all makes it enormously important to develop utility elicitation and optimization techniques that radically reduce the burden on the human participants. This is a large topic, but we have been exploring some promising avenues that include using hypervolumes to reduce the utility elicitation burden from humans, using information on the interdependencies between questions to reduce the amount of search required by optimization, and using LLMs to infer question interdependencies as well as offload to some extent the initial assessment of answers [32, 33].

4.8 Barrier: Tradeoff opacity

Tradeoff opacity refers to the fact that selecting the best answers from a large corpus can be difficult for decision makers because the tradeoffs may not be readily visible among the sea of answers, arguments and ratings. Highlighting the pareto-front in a utility diagram represents a highly effective way to visualize tradeoffs among candidate answers, but challenges remain when this is applied to scalable deliberation contexts. For example, the tradeoffs concerning how different stakeholder groups benefit from the answers may not be obvious. We could potentially solve this if we elicit enough detailed information on the raters to determine which stakeholder perspective they represent. But this can be problematic because providing anonymity to deliberation participants is generally very useful in terms of enabling honest feedback from the crowd. What can we do about this?

4.8.1 Solution: Stakeholder analysis

Our current approach to this challenge is to apply dimensionality reduction and clustering to the ratings the crowd gave to the answers and arguments. Each cluster will then represent a subset of the community that agree substantially in terms of how much they like different answers as well as why. A utility graph with the pareto front highlighted can be used to display the tradeoffs in terms of how the stakeholder groups gain and lose for each candidate answer. A "diff" capability can highlight *why* the groups differ, in terms of which arguments they each find compelling. We can then present this information to decision makers in the "select" phase so they can think, in a well-informed way, about which answers to select in order to maximize the alignment of the community during the implementation process.

5. Summary

The goal of this paper has been to explore how AI, particularly LLMs, can help us achieve effective deliberation at scale. Our method has been to systematically enumerate the *goals* that an ideal deliberation should achieve, the *barriers* that, in our observation, have most stymied the achievement of those goals, as well as some possible AI (especially LLM)-based *solutions* to overcoming these barriers. Here is a summary of that journey (**Figure 8**).

In doing this work, we arrived at a number of strategic insights that now inform our research:

- *The pivotal impact of LLMs*: LLMs can help address, in meaningful ways, all the critical barriers to scalable deliberation we have identified so far. This represents, in our opinion, an epochal shift, because many of these barriers have resisted solution for many years.

- *A division of labor:* the creativity and specificity gaps discussed above imply that an effective scalable deliberation system should implement a "division of labor" where AI and humans each contribute what they do best. AI is unmatched for large-scale data analysis, and LLMs are unmatched for their breadth of

goal: good documentation
  barrier: disorganized content
    solution: the unbundler
goal: excellent ideation
  barrier: crypto-content
    solution: content re-statement
  barrier: shallow answers
    solution: pregnant questions
    solution: creativity cues
    solution: contextualizer
goal: comprehensive critiques
  barrier: argument paucity
    solution: argument structure advisor
    solution: lemon agents
goal: accurate filtering
  barrier: rating paucity
    solution: answer clustering
goal: maximal efficiency
  barrier: haphazard effort allocation
    solution: user models
    solution: answer search optimization
    solution: VOI assessment optimization
  barrier: noise
    solution: semantic filtering
goal: correct selection
  barrier: tradeoff opacity
    solution: stakeholder pareto analysis

Figure 8.
Summary of goals barriers and solutions.

knowledge and sheer scale of semantic processing capability. Humans on the other hand remain superior in terms of applying specialized/localized knowledge and in creating truly new ideas. More specifically:

- *Moderation:* LLMs have proven capable of structuring disorganized human content in a way that means none of it is "lost in the pile," and at semantic filtering of noisy content. We also believe that they will be able, in concert with data science and optimization techniques, to efficiently guide large deliberations toward pareto-optimal answers.

- *Ideation*: We can use LLMs to provide idea seeds and pregnant questions, but should engage people in selecting and creatively proposing/refining/recombining answers.

- *Critiquing*: We can use LLMs to identify generic answer/argument weaknesses, but should rely on people for critiques that require local specialized and tacit knowledge.

- *Filtering:* LLMs should be used only with care, because of the still-unresolved issues with formally capturing the complexity of real-world utility functions.

- *Reporting:* LLMs and data science techniques can be used to dispel the opacity of the tradeoffs being made when selecting among large crowd-generated answer sets.

• *A shared deliberative framework:* We have found it very useful to use a uniform deliberative framework to mediate the interaction of people and AI, where both contribute in the same ways (i.e., by proposing answers, adding critiques, and so on). This allows us to plug in new AI capabilities as they emerge without re-architecting the system. It also requires that LLMs make their reasoning *transparent* (through the use of arguments), which helps address one of the major concerns of relying on them for decision-making.

6. Next steps

This paper represents work in progress. The GBS analysis we performed, for example, is no doubt incomplete: there are probably more normative goals, more barriers, and (probably many) more possible solutions for these barriers. Our analysis to date has focused the barriers we have observed in our own or others' real-world deliberation engagements but, of course, this is a tiny fraction of the group deliberations that occur world-wide on a daily basis.

We aspire to continue creatively developing and rigorously testing our solutions in realistic large-scale deliberation contexts. Our process is to first evolve the solutions on a rapid-prototyping version of the Deliberatorium, and then transfer the solutions that we judge mature enough to the commercial-quality version which is used for our real-world deliberation engagements with companies, universities, and other organizations.

It is possible of course that future developments in LLMs will change the calculus behind our research strategy. For example, the cost of fine-tuning LLMs may drop enough that it becomes practical for most organizations to create LLMs populated with the deep knowledge of their context needed to address the specificity gap. This could fundamentally change the AI/human division of labor.

Despite these limitations, we hope that this paper will help researchers broaden and deepen their image of how they can help achieve effective deliberation at scale, as well as to give participants and facilitators some sense of what the future may hold for how they will deliberate in partnership with AI systems.

Acknowledgements

The author would like to gratefully acknowledge the contributions made by Abhay Gupta, Arnab Sircar, David Babatunde, Habib Elhousseini, Lex Paulson, Manal El Akrouchi, Obiabuchi Nnanna, Oscar Hountondji, Paul Adubi, Rasheed Oyewole, and Samia Cherif. The author also gratefully acknowledges the generous financial support of the UM6P Vision 2030 program.

Author details

Mark Klein[1,2]

1 UM6P School for Collective Intelligence, Rabat, Morocco

2 MIT Center for Collective Intelligence, Cambridge, MA, USA

*Address all correspondence to: m_klein@mit.edu

References

[1] Shirky C. Here Comes Everybody: The Power of Organizing without Organizations. New York: Penguin; 2009

[2] Tapscott D, Williams AD. Wikinomics: How Mass Collaboration Changes Everything. New York: Portfolio Hardcover; 2006

[3] Jeppesen LB, Lakhani KR. Marginality and problem-solving effectiveness In broadcast search. Organization Science. 2010;**21**(5):1016-1033

[4] Gulley N. Patterns of innovation: A web-based MATLAB programming contest. In: Chi '01 Extended Abstracts on Human Factors in Computing Systems. Seattle, Washington: ACM; 2001. pp. 337-338. DOI: 10.1145/634067.634266

[5] Condorcet J-A-NDCMD. Condorcet: Foundations of Social Choice and Political Theory. Aldershot, Hampshire, England: Edward Elgar Publishing; 1994

[6] Surowiecki J. The Wisdom of Crowds. New York: Anchor; 2005

[7] Raymond E. The cathedral and the bazaar. Knowledge, Technology, and Policy. 1999;**12**(3):23-49

[8] Klein M, Dellarocas C, Rodriguez-Aguilar JA. A knowledge-based methodology for designing robust multi-agent systems. In: Proceedings from Autonomous Agents and Multi-Agent Systems; Bologna Italy. New York, USA: ACM Press; 2002

[9] Simon HA. The Sciences of the Artificial. Cambridge, MA, USA: MIT Press; 1996

[10] Eemeren FHV, Grootendorst R. A Systematic Theory of Argumentation: The Pragma-Dialectical Approach. Cambridge, England: Cambridge University Press; 2003

[11] Lawson B. How Designers Think. London: Routledge; 2006. DOI: 10.4324/9780080454979

[12] Mas-Colell A, Whinston MD, Green JR. Microeconomic Theory. New York, USA: Oxford University Press; 1995

[13] Klein M, Convertino G. An embarrassment of riches: A critical review of open innovation systems. Communications of the ACM. 2014;**57**(11):40-42. DOI: 10.1145/2629560

[14] Klein M. Towards crowd-scale deliberation. SSRN Electronic Journal. Jan 2017. DOI: 10.2139/Ssrn.2987624. Available from: https://www.researchgate.net/publication/328470119

[15] Klein M, Majdoubi N. The medium is the message: Toxicity declines in structured vs unstructured online deliberations. World Wide Web. 2024;**27**(31):1-18. DOI: 10.1007/S11280-024-01269-0

[16] Shum SJB, Selvin AM, Sierhuis M, Conklin J, Haley CB. Hypermedia support for argumentation-based rationale: 15 years on from gIBIS and QOC. In: Dutoit AH, Mccall R, Mistrik I, Paech B, editors. Rationale Management in Software Engineering. Berlin: Springer-Verlag; 2006

[17] Carr CS. Using computer supported argument visualization to teach legal argumentation. In: Kirschner PA, Shum SJB, Carr CS, editors. Visualizing Argumentation: Software Tools for Collaborative and Educational Sense-Making. London: Springer-Verlag; 2003. pp. 75-96

[18] Klein M. How to Harvest Collective Wisdom for Complex Problems: An Introduction to the MIT Deliberatorium. 2007. Available from: https://www.researchgate.net/publication/316659681

[19] Klein M. The MIT Deliberatorium: Enabling Large-Scale Deliberation about Complex Systemic Problems. 2011. Available from: https://www.researchgate.net/publication/221539673

[20] Babatunde DI, Nnanna O, Klein M. Moderating large scale online deliberative processes with large language models (LLMS): Enhancing collective decision-making. In: Proceedings from 40th ACM/SIGAPP Symposium on Applied Computing. New York, NY, USA: Association for Computing Machinery (ACM); 2025

[21] Page SE. The Difference: How the Power of Diversity Creates Better Groups, Firms, Schools, and Societies. Princeton, New Jersey, USA: Princeton University Press; 2008

[22] Singh S, Hndriks K, Heylen D, Baraka K. A systematic review of human-AI Co-creativity. Arxiv Preprint. 2025. Arxiv:2506.21333

[23] Wu Z, Ji D, Yu K, Zeng X, Wu D, Shidujaman M. AI creativity and the human-AI co-creation model. In: Human-Computer Interaction. Theory, Methods and Tools. Cham, Switzerland: Springer International Publishing; 2021

[24] Ge S, Huang S, Song X, Sun Y, Wang N, Qi K, et al. Comparing triz and brainstorming in human–agent design collaboration: Effects on cognitive processes and performance. Artificial Intelligence For Engineering Design, Analysis And Manufacturing. 2025;**39**:21. DOI: 10.1017/S0890060425100097

[25] Chiang C-W, Lu Z, Li Z, Yin M. Enhancing AI-assisted group decision making through LLM-powered devil's advocate. In: Proceedings of the 29th International Conference on Intelligent User Interfaces.New York, NY, USA: Association for Computing Machinery (ACM); 2024. DOI: 10.1145/3640543.3645199

[26] Lee S, Kim M, Hwang S, Kim D, Lee K. Amplifying minority voices: AI-mediated devil's advocate system for inclusive group decision-making. In: Proceedings of the 30th International Conference on Intelligent User Interfaces Companion (IUI Companion' 25). Cagliari, Italy. New York, NY, USA: ACM; 24-27 Mar 2025. p. 5. DOI: 10.1145/3708557.3716334

[27] Ma S, Chen Q, Wang X, Zheng C, Peng Z, Yin M, et al. Towards human-AI deliberation: Design and evaluation of LLM-empowered deliberative AI for AI-assisted decision-making. In: Proceedings of the 43rd ACM Conference on Human Factors in Computing Systems (CHI' 25), Yokohama, Japan, April 26-May 1, 2025. New York, NY, USA: Association for Computing Machinery (ACM); 2025. DOI: 10.1145/3706598.3713423

[28] Wang F, Li J, Zhu K, Jiang C. Inspiredebate: Multi-dimensional subjective-objective evaluation-guided reasoning and optimization for debating. Arxiv Preprint. 2025. Arxiv:2506.18102

[29] Klein M, Garcia ACB. High-speed idea filtering with the bag of lemons. Decision Support Systems. 2015;**78**:39-50. DOI: 10.1016/J.Dss.2015.06.005

[30] Klein M. Crowd-Scale Deliberation for Complex Problems: A Progress Report. Mar 2022. DOI: 10.13140/Rg.2.2.34676.01928. Available from:

https://www.researchgate.net/publication/359005729

[31] Klein M, Faratin P, Sayama H, Bar-Yam Y. Negotiating complex contracts. Group Decision and Negotiation. 2003;**12**(2):111-125

[32] Fujita K, Ito T, Klein M. Efficient issue-grouping approach for multiple interdependent issues negotiation between exaggerator agents. Decision Support Systems. 2014;**60**:10-17

[33] Klein M, Mohammed Y, Orden D. A Utility Function Compiler for Complex Negotiations. Jan 2025. DOI: 10.13140/RG.2.2.26659.31527. Available from: https://www.researchgate.net/publication/328470119

Chapter 4

Collective Superintelligence: Enabling Real-Time Conversational Deliberations among Humans and AI Agents at Unprecedented Scale

Louis B. Rosenberg

Abstract

This chapter explores the pursuit of Collective Superintelligence using a novel technology called Conversational Swarm Intelligence (CSI) that enables real-time conversational deliberations among human groups of potentially unlimited size. Traditional methods for capturing the Collective Intelligence (CI) of large groups use data aggregation techniques that are useful for narrow tasks such as numerical estimations and forecasting, but struggle to address the complex, open-ended problems faced by real-world organizations. CSI has overcome these limitations by adopting a dynamic systems approach inspired by the remarkable decision-making abilities of bee swarms, bird flocks, and fish schools. By leveraging the principles of Swarm Intelligence in combination with the power of Generative AI, CSI enables real-time conversational deliberations among networked human groups of potentially any size, empowering large teams to discuss issues, brainstorm ideas, debate alternatives, share knowledge, assess risks, and quickly converge on solutions with significantly amplified collective intelligence. This unlocks a new massively scalable framework for communication and collaboration. It also has the potential to enable large hybrid groups of human experts and AI agents to deliberate together in real-time and solve problems at collective intelligence levels that exceed all individual participants, both human and AI.

Keywords: collective superintelligence, swarm intelligence, conversational deliberation, conversational collective intelligence, generative AI, AI agents

1. Introduction

1.1 Why collective superintelligence (CS)?

The average Fortune 1000 company has over 30,000 employees and has large functional teams with many hundreds of members. Equally large teams exist in government, civil, scientific and defense organizations. And while many companies say that their most valuable asset is the intelligence and creativity of their teams, no technology exists to enable large teams to hold real-time conversations that allow them to leverage their collective knowledge, expertise, insight, sensibility and wisdom in optimized ways.

As will be described below, enabling productive real-time conversational deliberations among groups of *potentially unlimited size* could enable large organizations to efficiently solve complex problems with intelligence, insight, situational awareness, and creativity that significantly exceeds the abilities of all individual members.

In addition, many believe that AI agents will soon play a critical role in the global workforce, bringing their unique informational and analytical strengths to large teams. It is therefore important to consider not just enabling large human groups to hold thoughtful real-time deliberations but to also include AI agents within these deliberations at scale. In fact, research suggests we may be able to enable very large groups of human stakeholders and AI agents to amplify their collective intelligence to levels that significantly exceed all individual participants, both human and AI.

This goal is called Collective Superintelligence (CS) and this paper describes a recent technology called Conversational Swarm Intelligence (CSI) that has made significant progress in this direction. It merges the biological principle of Swarm Intelligence with the flexibility and power of Generative AI to enable productive conversational deliberations by text, voice, or video at *potentially unlimited scale*, and has been shown to significantly amplify the collective intelligence of collaborating teams [1].

1.2 Why scale conversational deliberation?

Collective Intelligence (CI) is the well-known principle that when large human groups combine their knowledge, expertise, and insights, they can outperform the median participant on a range of useful tasks [2]. This "amplification effect" has been shown to scale with group size, especially when members have diverse knowledge, expertise, perspectives, or situational awareness [3, 4].

The concept was famously discovered by Sir Francis Galton in 1906 when he asked 800 farmers to estimate the weight of an ox and found the median value was surprisingly accurate. That was over a century ago and yet today, most CI methods for large groups still aggregate data collected from individuals. While aggregating human insights is useful if you have 800 farmers and an ox whose weight you need to estimate, most organizations need to solve significantly more complex and open-ended problems, usually with interrelated tradeoffs, risk factors, contingencies and alternatives.

In real organizations, Conversational Deliberation (CD) is the fundamental method by which teams interactively share perspectives, brainstorm ideas, debate alternatives, assess risks, prioritize options, and converge on solutions that leverage their combined knowledge, wisdom, expertise, and situational awareness [5]. It has therefore been a longstanding goal of researchers to combine the *deliberative benefits* of real-time conversation with the *collective intelligence* benefits of very large groups.

Unfortunately, authentic real-time conversations do not scale. Research into conversational dynamics suggests that the ideal size for a thoughtful deliberation is only about 4–7 people [6, 7]. At this scale, each individual has a good amount of *airtime* to express their views and low *wait-time* to respond to others. But as group size grows, airtime decreases, wait-time increases, and conversational dynamics rapidly degrade. By 10–12 people, it ceases to be an interactive discussion, devolving into a series of monologs, and above 15–20 people, it becomes a one-to-many presentation [8, 9].

This has made it impossible to leverage the collective intelligence of large groups through natural deliberative conversations. Instead, the primary methods for harnessing the collective intelligence of large groups have involved capturing data from individual members through polls, surveys, or prediction markets and statistically aggregating to produce a combined result [2]. Such aggregation techniques are generally referred to as Wisdom of Crowds (WoC) and have been shown to outperform the median participant in certain tasks. That said, most CI methods have significant limitations:

i. Because traditional CI methods aggregate data instead of enabling true deliberations, they generally have *narrow use-cases* such as numeric estimation, probabilistic forecasting, and multiple-choice selection. In real-world organizations, complex problems often require open-ended brainstorming and debate among stakeholders to find solutions [10].

ii. Because traditional CI systems aggregate preference data, they often fail to reveal the *underlying reasons why* the group favors or rejects the various options under consideration. Often, the *reasons why* contain the most useful insights, especially when surfaced through deliberation.

iii. Because traditional CI systems aggregate data, they generally converge on the *most popular perspective* within a group. This often fails when the "conventional wisdom" is flawed [11]. This problem is common in close-knit teams that develop *organizational conventional wisdom*.

iv. Many CI methods use sequential upvoting methods in online forums or sequential "trades" in online prediction markets. Both methods are highly susceptible to social influence bias (i.e. *herding* or *snowballing*) in which prior upvotes or trades significantly influence future upvotes or trades. This amplifies noise [12, 13] and causes momentum distortions (i.e. bubbles) that dampen intelligence [14].

v. The goal of CI should not be to beat the *median participant*, but to outperform *all participants*. This is rarely achieved by WoC methods that converge on the most popular solution, not the best solution [15].

vi. The future of CI will likely include humans and AI agents [16]. Without group deliberations among large human and AI teams, there is no path for human sensibilities to organically guide hybrid solutions [15].

Overall, aggregation-based CI methods have useful applications but generally do not support the complex, open-ended problems faced by real organizations. As will be described in the next section, CSI aims to address these barriers by combining the *intelligence amplification* of large groups with the *deliberative power* of natural real-time conversations [17, 18]. In addition, CSI supports deliberations among large "hybrid groups" of humans and AI agents, further expanding the effectiveness of conversation-based collective intelligence [16–18]. Together, these benefits suggest that CSI may be a viable pathway for enabling human groups and AI agents to collaborate on complex real-world challenges and collectively exceed the intelligence levels and problem-solving abilities of all members, both human and AI. This objective is called Collective Superintelligence [16].

2. From biological swarms to conversational swarms

Before reviewing the methods of Conversational Swarm Intelligence (CSI), it is useful to cover the biological principle of Swarm Intelligence (SI) that inspired the methods and describe a predecessor technology for leveraging SI among large networked human groups, Artificial Swarm Intelligence (ASI).

2.1 Swarm intelligence (SI)

For over a century, scientists have observed that natural species can amplify their group intelligence by forming real-time systems among members. This phenomenon is commonly referred to as Swarm Intelligence (SI) and it enables a wide range of social organisms, from schooling fish and swarming bees to flocking birds, to solve problems together that are beyond the intellectual capacity of the individual members [19]. These natural systems do not aggregate data like many large human groups but instead form real-time systems in which members "deliberate" by interactively pulling for various alternatives until the group finds a solution that maximizes their collective support.

Honeybees, for example, can collectively solve complex problems such as choosing the optimal location for a new home site from among many candidate sites. They do this by vibrating their bodies in support of various options until the group converges on the solution that maximizes their collective support [20]. This vibration-based deliberation among bees is called a "waggle dance" (because it looks like the bees are dancing) and has been shown to engender an optimized decision-making process that greatly exceeds the mental capacity of the individual bees that comprise the system [21].

Even more surprising, the deliberative systems formed by honeybees follow a similar decision-making process to neurological brains [22]. Both brains and swarms contain large numbers of *excitable processing units* (i.e., neurons and bees) that work in parallel to (a) integrate noisy data, (b) weigh competing alternatives and (c) converge on preferred solutions. In both brains and swarms, outcomes emerge through real-time competition among sub-groups of excitable units. When one sub-group exceeds a threshold level of support, a decision emerges [23, 24].

The similarities between the role of *neurons* in brains and the role of *members* in swarms inspired early researchers to refer to Swarm Intelligence as a *"brain of brains"* and to explore swarm-based models as a path to Collective Superintelligence [25]. This led to Artificial Swarm Intelligence (ASI) in 2014, which was the first swarm-based technology for amplifying collective intelligence [22].

2.2 Artificial swarm intelligence (ASI)

Artificial Swarm Intelligence (ASI) was developed in 2014 to enable networked human groups of potentially any size to deliberate as real-time systems modeled on the dynamics of bee swarms [25]. The first studies of ASI were conducted using an online platform called UNU that provided each user with a graphical magnet to vary the direction and magnitude of their sentiments during real-time deliberations. Intelligent algorithms monitor the motion of each participant's magnet in real-time and uses the dynamics to infer relative conviction within the group. As participants adjust their magnets in response to each other, swarming algorithms update the speed and direction of a collectively controlled puck until the group targets a selected outcome together [26].

Using UNU and successor platforms like SWARM, researchers have studied ASI extensively over the last decade for a wide range of applications ranging from group decision-making and financial forecasting to medical diagnosis. For example, researchers at Oxford University and Unanimous AI published a study in 2017 showing that groups of financial traders, when deliberating as real-time swarms, could amplify their forecasting accuracy by 36% ($p < 0.001$) [26].

Similarly, researchers at Stanford and Unanimous AI published an NSF-funded study showing that small groups of doctors could diagnose chest x-rays as real-time swarms and reduced their diagnostic errors by 33% compared to traditional methods [27, 28]. Studies at California Polytechnic showed "swarming" groups could significantly increase their "social sensitivity" and "social perceptiveness" in subjective judgment tasks [29, 30]. Other studies show significant benefits when groups use ASI to prioritize goals, forecast events, and find socially optimal solutions to ethical challenges or political charged issues [31–33].

Overall, enabling human groups to deliberate as real-time swarms has many advantages over aggregation-based CI methods. That said, ASI also has limitations. For example, graphical swarms have proven most effective for narrow tasks such as numerical estimations, probabilistic forecasting, multiple-choice selection and itemized prioritization. The desire to expand beyond this narrow range of uses has motivated ASI researchers to explore new methods that combine the interactive benefits of *swarming* with the open-ended flexibility of conversational deliberation.

2.3 Conversational swarm intelligence (CSI)

It has been a longstanding goal in the field of collective intelligence to combine the *deliberative power* of natural real-time conversation with the *intelligence amplification* of very large human groups. As described in Section 1.2 above, real-time conversations are inherently unscalable because each member's airtime drops and wait-time increases with each additional participant. A technological solution was therefore required.

In 2023, researchers published the first studies showing that productive real-time conversations among networked human groups could be conducted at potentially unlimited scales and that scaling-up deliberations can significantly amplify collective intelligence [1, 17, 18]. The resulting technology is called Conversational Swarm Intelligence (CSI). It leverages prior learnings from research into ASI technology (based on the dynamics of bee swarms) and expands the conceptual models using the dynamics of fish schools [1, 10, 34].

As background, fish schools are often called "Super Organisms" because they can quickly make critical decisions despite each member having *incomplete information* and most members having limited *situational awareness*. To illustrate this, **Figure 1** below shows a large school facing a theoretical life-or-death situation in which three predators approach from three directions. As portrayed, no individual has *sufficient information* or wide enough *situational awareness* to find an optimal solution.

In fact, most members have no direct awareness of any threats, and only three subsets of members (circled below) are aware of a single threat. This is analogous to human organizations that often face complex real-world problems in which subgroups have limited information, specialized expertise, and narrow situational awareness.

Figure 1.
A large fish school faces a complex life-or-death problem.

2.3.1 So how do fish schools solve this?

Schooling fish evolved the ability to "deliberate" among small groups of nearby fish using a specialized organ called a *lateral line*. This organ detects pressure and vibration changes in the water around them to monitor the *directional intentions* of their neighbors. Because each small group of neighbors overlaps other small groups of neighbors, the local deliberations can rapidly propagate information throughout the full population as shown in **Figure 2**. This allows thousands of fish to quickly deliberate in unison and converge on optimized decisions [35].

2.3.2 Can humans form a swarm intelligence conversationally?

Inspired by fish schools, Conversational Swarm Intelligence works by dividing large, networked groups into overlapping subgroups, each containing about 4–7 members (an ideal size for real-time conversations). Of course, people do not

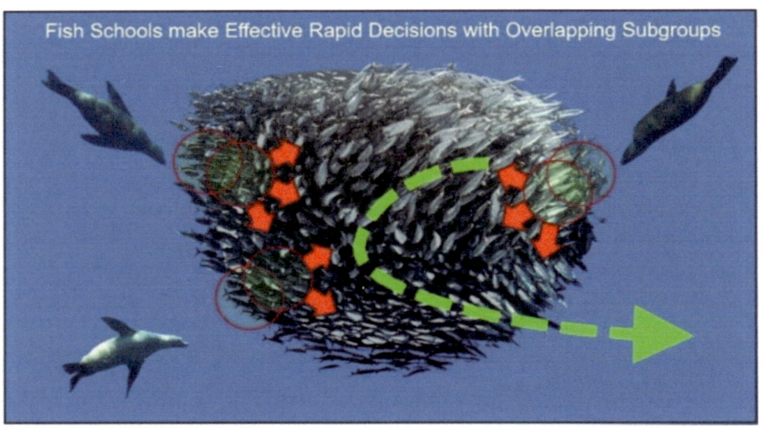

Figure 2.
A collective solution quickly propagates through the fish school.

possess the fish-like ability to deliberate in overlapping subgroups. In fact, we are unable to focus on multiple conversations at once. This is called the "cocktail party problem" because at cocktail parties many small groups form in close proximity. If you are engaged in a small group conversation at a party and shift your attention to the discussion within a neighboring group, you are likely to struggle to follow either conversation [36].

To address this, CSI uses Large Language Models (LLMs) to deploy an innovative AI agent called a *"Conversational Surrogate"* [1, 10, 16–18, 37, 38]. After CSI divides a large human group into a set of small subgroups, it automatically inserts a Surrogate Agent into each one. This agent is designed to: (a) observe the local deliberation in its subgroup, (b) distill key insights in real time, and (c) pass those insights to other subgroups where that group's local *Surrogate Agent* will express the insights to its members as *natural dialog*. This weaves all subgroups together into a single unified conversation (of potentially any size) in which the full population can discuss issues, brainstorm ideas, evaluate options, and efficiently converge on collective solutions.

Figure 3 below shows an example CSI architecture in which a 100-person group is divided into 14 parallel subgroups, each subgroup having seven or eight human members and one AI agent. This creates a single large conversation in which ideas, insights, assessments, and rationales rapidly propagate until the group converges on one or more solutions that maximize the population's collective confidence or conviction.

It is important to note that Surrogate Agents do not bring outside information into the conversation. Instead, they only pass information between local groups by representing the knowledge, views, or insights of one or more human participants. In addition, the Surrogate Agents are designed to modulate the wording and emphasis of their language to convey the strength of local sentiments as they propagate content across groups.

Also, unlike fish schools, for which groups overlap by virtue of proximity, CSI is often configured to enable all subgroups to *overlap simultaneously*. This takes nature's basic concept of a "swarm" and turns it into a "hyperswarm" that is significantly more efficient than the biology that inspired it [39, 40]. Thus, CSI enables very large groups to hold real-time conversations that quickly leverage their collective knowledge, wisdom, insights, and expertise, and can rapidly converge on optimized solutions.

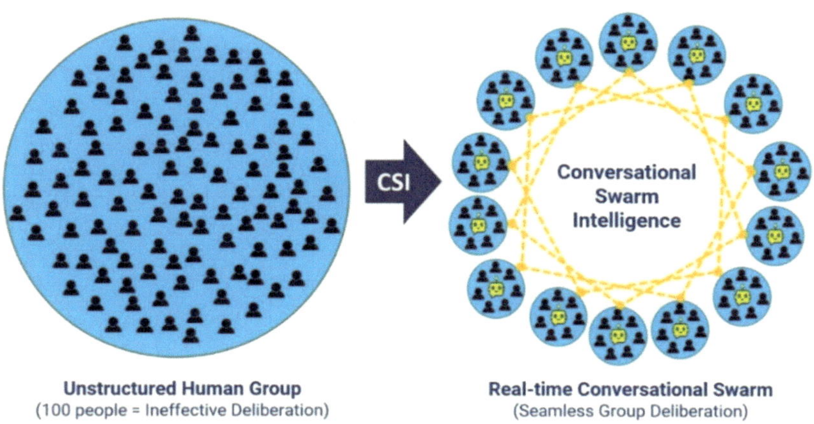

Figure 3.
CSI enables large, networked human groups to hold real-time conversations using LLM-powered Surrogate Agents *that enable all of the groups to overlap in real-time.*

In addition, CSI has inherent benefits that amplify collective intelligence by diffusing the influence of *loudmouth bias*, *authority bias*, and *first-talker bias*, which can significantly distort traditional deliberations. For example, because CSI divides a large group into overlapping subgroups, a single strong personality or authority figure (i.e., a loudmouth) can only have an oversized impact within their local subgroup. For an idea, insight, or perspective expressed by a loudmouth to propagate, it must stand on its own deliberative merits when expressed in other subgroups by a Surrogate Agent.

Similarly, the *first ideas expressed* during a group conversation (large or small) can have an oversized impact on the direction of the deliberation and the ideas that surface. CSI solves this. For example, **Figure 3** above shows a CSI structure with 14 parallel conversations. This means 14 different "first ideas" will be expressed in real-time, each of which must not only gain support within its local group, but it must also compete with the ideas emerging from other groups to propagate throughout the swarm.

Thus, CSI not only allows conversations to scale, it drives *smarter outcomes* by enabling many ideas to surface and percolate in parallel, with the most compelling insights spreading fastest, while the weakest points gradually fade away.

2.4 Validation studies of CSI

A number of studies have been performed to assess the ability of CSI systems to enable effective real-time conversations among large, networked groups, and to significantly amplify collective intelligence. These studies use an online cloud-based CSI platform called Thinkscape® that is accessible to users through standard web-browsers, requires no training for participants, and enables real-time conversations among up to 400 users at once. The platform currently supports text-chat and voice-to-text dialog, and can share media such as images, videos, spreadsheets, or webpages, to all participants.

2.4.1 Groupwise estimation study

In a 2023 study, researchers replicated a classic CI experiment in which large groups were asked to estimate the number of gumballs in a jar [1]. Groups of approximately 240 participants were tested in three scenarios: (i) as individuals filling out a survey, (ii) as aggregated estimates across surveys, and (iii) as a "conversational swarm" using a CSI platform (Thinkscape) that partitioned the 240 participants into 47 subgroups of five or six human members and a single Surrogate Agent. The results showed CSI groups had an average estimation error of 12% which was significantly more accurate than the average individual (55% error) and the traditional CI aggregation method (25% error).

2.4.2 Collective IQ study

In a 2024 study conducted by researchers at Carnegie Mellon University and Unanimous AI, groups of 35 participants were given standardized IQ tests using the Thinkscape CSI platform. The results showed that groups using CSI could hold thoughtful deliberative conversations to collectively efficiently answer the IQ questions. The test groups using CSI scored an average IQ in the *97th percentile* (IQ = 128). As shown in **Figure 4**, this score significantly outperformed the median individual

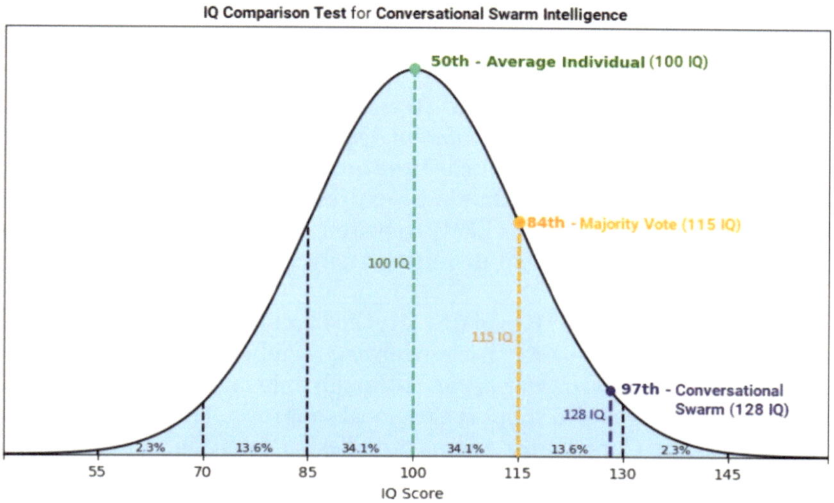

Figure 4.
Results of collective IQ Test study comparing CSI to traditional methods.

in each group (IQ = 100) and significantly outperformed a traditional aggregation-based CI method (IQ = 115) [10].

2.4.3 Large-scale brainstorming study

In another study conducted by researchers at Unanimous AI and Carnegie Mellon, groups of 75 participants were given a standardized brainstorming test known as an Alternative Use Task (AUT). Specifically, participants were asked to collaboratively brainstorm ideas for unconventional uses of common objects with the goal of allowing a surplus of those objects to be sold by a fictional company. Groups were tested in two scenarios: (a) by holding a real-time conversation in a single large chat room similar to Microsoft Teams or Google Chat or (b) by holding a real-time conversation using the Thinkscape CSI platform described above.

All participants were required to brainstorm using each of two test scenarios. Participants were then asked to compare their experiences. The results showed that participants greatly preferred brainstorming using CSI, with a significant majority reporting that the brainstorming process was *more productive*, *more collaborative*, and *surfaced better solutions* when using CSI. In addition, a significant majority of brainstorming participants reported *feeling more heard* and *feeling more ownership* when using CSI [41].

3. Hybrid conversational swarm intelligence (HyCSI)

3.1 Enabling hybrid conversational groups of humans and AI agents

Thus far we have reviewed how CSI enables large human groups to hold productive conversations at scale and can amplify collective intelligence. The next step toward unlocking the potential of Collective Superintelligence is to bring additional AI agents into the CSI architecture. The goal is not to replace human stakeholders, but for AI to serve a supporting role by providing each subgroup with relevant *factual information*, *analytical insights*, and *logical arguments* for consideration during their deliberations.

To achieve these goals, a new type of AI agent was developed for inclusion in the CSI model. Referred to as a "*Contributor Agent,*" the functionality is aimed at observing each local deliberation in real-time and assessing if and when factual, analytical, or logical information should be expressed that (a) has not yet been discussed in that subgroup, and (b) is likely to be relevant and helpful to the ongoing discussion, either by supporting or disputing an idea or alternative that is currently being debated.

Figure 5 shows an example Hybrid CSI (HyCSI) architecture in which each of the parallel subgroups contains six or seven human members and is supported by *one Surrogate Agent* and *one Contributor Agent*. Although only one is shown, CSI can use multiple Contributor Agents to support each local subgroup. This can be valuable if each of the supporting Contributor Agents provides information, expertise, or insight from a different perspective. In addition, CSI can be structured as a hierarchy of increasingly larger subgroups (i.e., swarms of swarms) for mass scaling purposes [42].

It is important to stress the benefit of deploying an independent Contributor Agent in each of the parallel local subgroups in the Hybrid CSI structure. Referring back to **Figure 5** below, the example shows 14 parallel subgroups, each supported by a separate Contributor Agent that provides distinct information to its subgroup that is unique in content, timing, and expression as compared to the Contributor Agents in other groups. This provides *factual diversity* across subgroups, enabling the population to consider a wide range of details in parallel, with the most impactful factual content likely gaining support by spreading between subgroups while the least valuable content fades away.

This ensures that contributions by AI agents, like the contributions of human members, propagate based on *deliberative value*. This leverages the informational power of AI agents but maintains human control over the deliberative process.

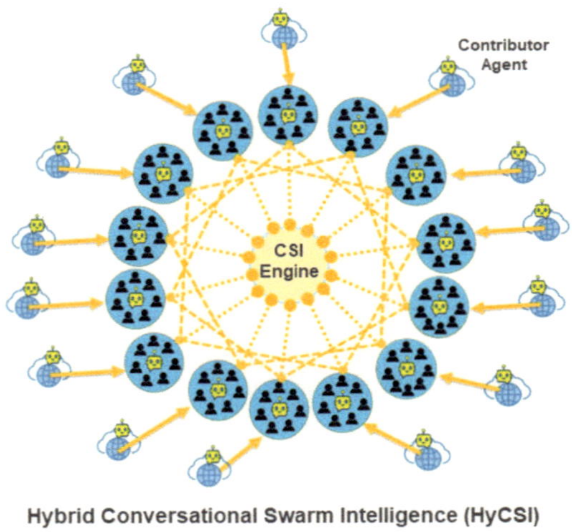

Figure 5.
A hybrid CSI structure is shown with human members and contributor AI agents.

3.2 Validation of hybrid CSI

In 2024, researchers published the first studies in which hybrid groups of human stakeholders and Contributor Agents deliberated together in real-time. As described below, the studies evaluated the usefulness of Contributor Agents designed to provide factual information during groupwise decision-making tasks.

3.2.1 Hybrid decision-making study

In a 2024 study of Hybrid Conversational Swarm Intelligence, networked groups of twenty-give sports fans were tasked with deliberating to collaboratively field Fantasy Baseball teams for competition in a public daily fantasy contest [16]. While fantasy sports may seem frivolous, it is a good model for organizational decision-making because it requires *subject-matter expertise,* probabilistic *forecasting skills*, and the ability to *strategically allocate funds*. That's because each 25-person group was given a fixed payroll to spend on multiple players.

The experiment was run weekly for 10 consecutive weeks and scored using standard fantasy baseball rules. Using the online CSI platform called Thinkscape, the 25 person groups were automatically split into five subgroups, each containing five human members, one Surrogate Agent, and one Contributor Agent. The contributor agents were specifically designed to provide *factual information* about Major League Baseball, including relevant statistics about various players and teams [16].

The results showed that 25-person groups using CSI amplified their performance to the *73rd percentile* (among members who averaged in the 50th percentile). More importantly, when asked to assess the usefulness of the Contributor Agents (called *Infobots* in the study), *87% of participants* supported the statement: *"Our decisions were stronger because of information provided by the Infobot."*

4. Enabling video deliberations at unlimited scale

In the pursuit of Collective Superintelligence, the natural next step for CSI platforms is to expand from real-time text and voice to real-time videoconferencing. In addition, innovative methods are needed for enabling asynchronous engagement as it becomes logistically more difficult to gather groups simultaneously at larger and larger scale.

4.1 Can CSI enable videoconferencing at massive scales?

To enable productive video conversations at very large scale, a next-generation CSI architecture has been developed in which large groups are divided into parallel video-conferencing subgroups, each of which is provided with a Surrogate Agent that appears as an embodied participant (i.e., as an animated avatar.) As shown in **Figure 6** below, the animated avatar performs the surrogate functions described in Section 2.3 above by receiving insights extracted from other local groups and expressing those insights as natural dialog within its own group. This weaves all of the local deliberations together into a unified conversation, enabling the full population to collectively discuss issues, debate alternatives, brainstorm ideas, prioritize options, and converge on groupwise solutions.

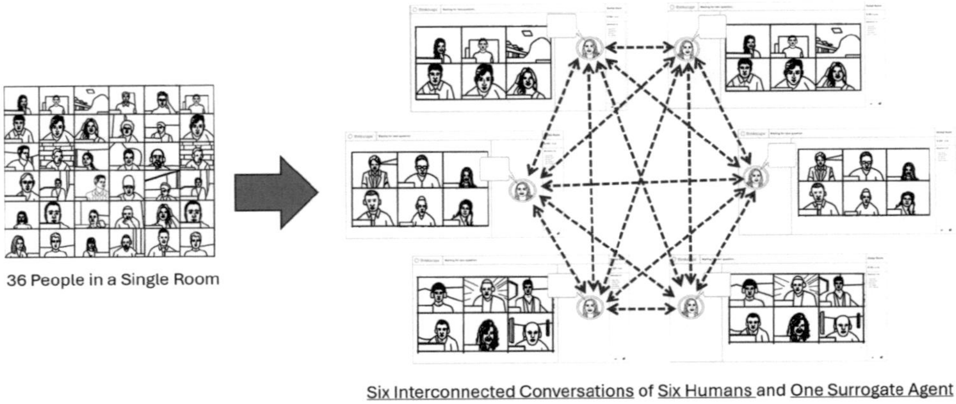

Figure 6.
Example CSI architecture for real-time video-conferencing among 36 people.

While the above figure shows a real-time video conference among 36 individuals, the same structure can be used for hundreds or thousands of participants. Also, hierarchical structures for CSI have been developed (i.e. swarms of swarms) that enable scaling at much larger group sizes. Also, one or more Contributor Agents can be added to each local room as additional avatars to bring relevant informational content into the group dialogs as discussed in Section 3.1 above. In this way, very large groups of human participants and AI agents can deliberate in large-scale video conversations in which they discuss issues, brainstorm ideas, debate alternatives and converge on solutions that maximize their collective conviction.

4.2 Can CSI support asynchronous participation?

By definition, groupwise conversational deliberation is a synchronous social experience in which the participants have the opportunity to react to points made by colleagues as they emerge, enabling groups to build upon each other's ideas, debate supporting or opposing arguments in real-time, and consider a wide variety of opinions, perspectives and rationales as they debate issues. That said, synchrony imposes significant logistical constraints upon teams as it requires large groups to coordinate specific times for deliberative activities. This can be challenging for groups that span diverse geographies, workflows, and time-zones.

For these reasons, asynchronous tools like polls, surveys, forums, and prediction markets have logistical strengths vs. synchronous methods. Unfortunately, those logistical strengths often come with significant limitations that hinder collective intelligence and hamper authentic cross-pollination of insights. As described in Section 1.2 above, when ideas and arguments are contributed sequentially in forums, prediction markets, and other tools that engage participants over time, *temporal bias* and *social influence bias* can significantly amplify noise and distort outcomes. This is because ideas expressed early in an asynchronous process can get overweighted consideration, not because of their merits but because of their timing. In addition, ideas that receive early support by an asynchronous upvote become more likely to receive additional upvotes.

Such "momentum" effects in forums and markets hinder collective intelligence. In a well-known study conducted at MIT, Hebrew University, and NYU, researchers studied the impact of a random *first upvote* on online forums and found that it increased the likelihood of future positive ratings by 32% and caused herding effects that distorted the final ratings by 25% [12]. We can infer similar temporal herding effects in asynchronous messaging tools.

In addition, asynchronous messaging platforms like Slack, Discord, and Microsoft Teams have been found to overwhelm collaborating members due to the frequent notifications and interruptions, and the pressure of growing backlogs of messages, leading to stress and reduced productivity [43–46]. In addition, the growing backlog of sequential messages in platforms like Slack can cause their own temporal biasing effects and can drive uneven participation that distorts outcomes [47].

This begs the question – *Can we combine the deliberative benefits of real-time conversation with the logistical benefits of asynchronous engagement?* One solution that leverages the innovations of CSI is to enable *later participants* to engage with Surrogate Agents that represent the perspectives of earlier participants [48]. To enable this without temporal biasing or social biasing, the CSI architecture can be structured to enable *sequential batches* of members who participate synchronously and introduce time-based Surrogate Agents that represent views and opinions surfaced in prior batches. This is shown schematically in **Figure** 7 below.

The example above shows a first networked human group of 100 participants holding a real-time conversation using a CSI structure that divides them into 14 subgroups interconnected by Surrogate Agents to form a unified deliberation. Then, at a future moment in time, a second batch of 100 participants engage in a synchronous conversation, also shown as 14 subgroups woven together by Surrogate Agents. In addition, each subgroup in the second batch has a second Surrogate Agent that represents ideas, views, and perspectives that were surfaced in the first batch. As shown, any number of additional batches can be conducted over time with Surrogate Agents added that represent all prior batches. In this way, the conversation is woven together over time but is done at sufficient parallel scale to avoid momentum effects (i.e. herding) that distorts forums, markets, and other traditional asynchronous collaboration methods.

In addition, it should be noted that at each stage in the process, the CSI structure can also include Contributor Agents that bring informational content into the deliberations, thereby enabling groups of human members and AI agents to collaborate conversationally in real-time batches, combining their collective insights asynchronously over time.

In addition, if we ensure that "seed population" (i.e. first batch) is large enough, the subsequent batches can be relatively small and still avoid temporal biasing and social biasing impacts. In fact, the subsequent batches could be scaled down to single

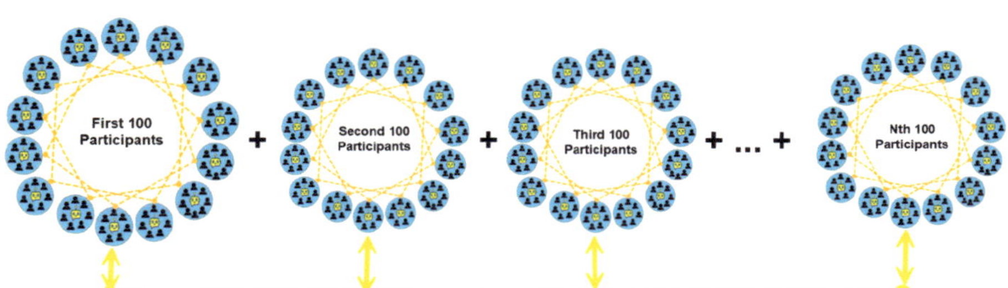

Figure 7.
Example CSI architecture semi-synchronous deliberations at unlimited scale.

deliberative groups (e.g., 4–7 people) or could be scaled down further to a single individual engaging with one or more Surrogate Agents. These options for asynchronous engagement over time are illustrated in **Figure 8** below.

To avoid the traditional problems of asynchronous engagement a sufficiently large seed population is recommended in the first batch [49]. That said, once a large enough deliberation has occurred, single individuals can engage directly with a single Surrogate Agent that represents the views, opinions, and or perspectives surfaced in prior deliberations. Such a *Pluribus Agent* is a personified embodiment of the collective intelligence at that moment in time. A single individual can therefore interview this emergent collective intelligence, or even argue with it, by holding a real-time interactive conversation with an animated *Pluribus Avatar* that represents the prior deliberations.

In addition, if the population of prior participants is large enough, and if the prior deliberations included Contributor Agents that bring the informational and analytical power of AI into the conversations, the Pluribus Avatar could be a real-time representation of a Collective Superintelligence that can outperform all members, both human and AI, when solving complex real-world problems that require human oversight [40].

4.3 Why enable hybrid collective superintelligence?

As outlined above, the goal of Collective Superintelligence is to enable large human groups to collaboratively solve complex open-ended problems at intelligence levels that exceed all participating members. This would offer significant value for organizations, enabling teams of potentially any size to leverage their collective knowledge, wisdom, insights and expertise to quickly address critical issues. Such abilities would be particularly useful for tackling multifaceted problems that require input from a diverse range of disciplines and specialties and a broad spectrum of situational awareness.

In addition, there is a larger moral imperative for the pursuit of Collective Superintelligence stemming from the rapid advancement of AI systems. Many researchers expect AI agents will soon be widely deployed within organizations that can solve expert-level problems at speed, accuracy, and intelligence levels that surpass the abilities of most human employees [50–52]. Whether or not these AI agents achieve the definition of Artificial General Intelligence (AGI), when AI systems do reach a perceived state of *"Cognitive Supremacy"* with respect to human stakeholders, we could see a growing tendency for organizational managers to defer important decisions to automated agents under the assumption that AI systems have deeper

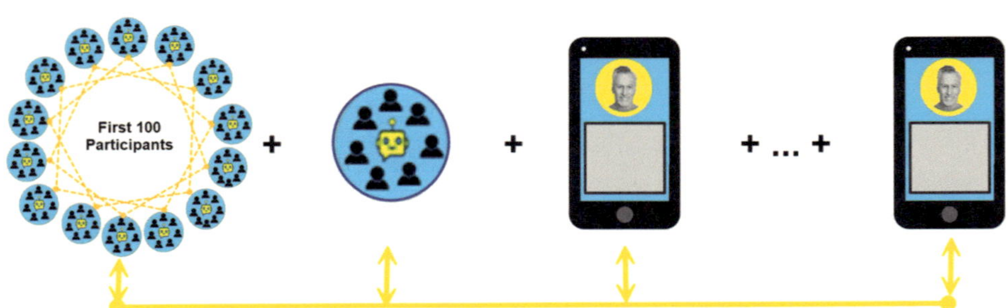

Figure 8.
Example CSI architecture semi-synchronous deliberations at various subsequent scales.

knowledge and stronger analytical skills [40]. This would be a dangerous direction for governance at all levels of management, as many critical decisions require not just sufficient knowledge and analytical prowess, but human values, morals, interests and sensibilities [53].

Thus, by enabling large human groups to form real-time deliberative systems in collaboration with AI agents, we may be able to foster a hybrid Collective Superintelligence that can solve complex organizational problems at intelligence levels that exceed all participants, both human and AI. In addition, such systems could help ensure that human values and societal interests remain inherent to the deliberative process.

4.4 What are the risks of hybrid collective superintelligence?

While CSI has potential to enable human deliberations at unlimited scale and to significantly amplify collective intelligence, we must consider the potential risks of enabling Surrogate Agents and Contributor Agents to participate within groupwise conversations. A significant risk of all human-AI interactions is the current tendency of participants to perceive information provided by AI agents as more *authoritative* or *accurate* than content from human members [54, 55]. This is sometimes referred to as "AI authority bias" and it can distort how humans reach decisions, form subjective judgments, or make forward-looking predictions.

To counter this effect within CSI and HyCSI systems, effort should be made to ensure that participants do not view the AI agents as *authority figures* within the groupwise deliberation. This means not giving the AI agents a "facilitator" or "moderator" role but instead designing the agents to contribute content using similar conversational tone, phrasing, and confidence as human participants [42].

In addition, it is important to remind human participants that the contributions made by Surrogate Agents in each local dialog were not formulated independently by an AI system but were derived based on real-time human discussions in other subgroups. In this way, the human participants are more likely to view the AI contributions with the same skepticism they would have if the comment had come directly from human members of the group. These reminders have been implemented in CSI systems in two ways:

First, the AI agents are generally designed to provide an "attribution indicator" next to their comments. These indicators inform participants of the subgroup(s) from which their comments were derived. In addition, CSI systems provide human participants with a graphical representation of the CSI network and the AI messages that are passed among subgroups. Such graphical reminders help ensure the human participants do not forget that the Surrogate Agents are sharing content between groups and not offering their own AI-generated opinions or perspectives. An example of such a graphical representation is shown below in **Figure 9**.

The figure above depicts a group of 102 participants broken into 21 small subgroups and uses animated "AI" icons to represent the real-time passing of ideas, arguments, counter arguments, and other content between subgroups. In addition, "connection traces" are left behind by the AI icons as they pass between groups, showing the growing network of connections during deliberations. These visual indicators remind the human participants that their group's conversation is deeply connected to the network of other groups and that the agents are acting as surrogates that merely share content between and among participants.

Beyond countering authority bias, additional protections should be put in place to ensure AI agents are not deliberately influencing or manipulating participants.

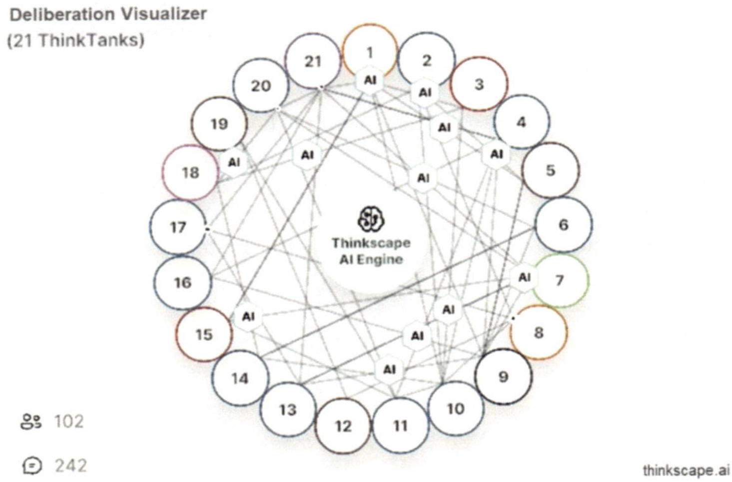

Figure 9.
Snapshot of animated "Deliberation Visualizer" in Thinkscape.ai CSI platform.

Often referred to as the AI Manipulation Problem, the danger is that AI agents could be deployed with super-human persuasive abilities [56]. This risk is present in all AI systems that use conversational agents and should be addressed through policy protections. In the absence of policy, the recommended solution is transparency that enables stakeholders to audit the AI contributions so they can ensure that AI agents accurately and objectively represented the views of subgroups [57]. These auditing abilities are currently present in CSI platforms and should be maintained.

5. Conclusions and future work

Conversational Swarm Intelligence (CSI) and its hybrid variant (HyCSI), offer a unique opportunity to enable real-time communication, collaboration, and collective problem-solving at unprecedented scales. This could provide significant value to large organizations that currently have no methods for conducting real-time conversational deliberations among large functional and cross-functional teams.

Future research should expand validation studies to diverse real-world applications, including strategic planning, organizational decision-making, policy deliberations, collaborative forecasting, civic engagement and deliberative democracy. In addition, studies should expand the size of collaborating groups from hundreds to many thousands of simultaneous members and assess the deliberative efficiency, decision-making effectiveness, analytical accuracy, and collective intelligence amplification.

In addition, future research should explore the logistical constraints caused by synchronous deliberations in real-world organizations and study the effectiveness of asynchronous CSI methods that employ Surrogate Agents to pass insights from subsequent individuals or subgroups to future individuals or subgroups as described in Section 4.2 above.

Also, future work should refine the abilities of Contributor Agents to provide domain-specific informational support while ensuring that human stakeholders maintain control over the deliberative process. Future work should also explore the ethical implications of large-scale hybrid deliberations among human members and AI agents, and work to protect human agency and autonomy.

And finally, research should explore the ability of CSI to enable large groups of humans and artificial agents to collaboratively solve problems at intelligence levels that exceed all individual members, both human and AI. This could enable large hybrid groups function as a Collective Superintelligence that inherently keeps human values, morals, interests, and sensibilities inherently in the loop.

Author details

Louis B. Rosenberg
Unanimous AI, Pismo Beach, California, USA

*Address all correspondence to: louis@unanimous.ai

References

[1] Rosenberg L, Willcox G, Schumann H. Towards collective superintelligence, a pilot study. In: 2023 International Conference on Human-Centered Cognitive Systems (HCCS). IEEE; 2023. pp. 1-6

[2] Riedl C, Kim YJ, Gupta P, Malone TW, Woolley AW. Quantifying collective intelligence in human groups. National Academy of Sciences of the United States of America. 2021;**118**(21):e2005737118

[3] Woolley AW, Aggarwal I, Malone TW. Collective intelligence and group performance. Current Directions in Psychological Science. 2015;**24**(6):420-424. DOI: 10.1177/0963721415599543

[4] Malone TW. Superminds: The Surprising Power of People and Computers Thinking Together, Amazon. Little, Brown and Company; 2019

[5] Nelson LM. Collaborative problem solving. In: Instructional-Design Theories and Models. Routledge; 2013. pp. 241-267

[6] Cooney G et al. The many minds problem: Disclosure in dyadic vs. group conversation. Current Opinion in Psychology. 2020;**31**:22-27. Special Issue on Privacy and Disclosure, Online and in Social Interactions edited by L. John, D. Tamir, M. Slepian

[7] Fay N, Garrod S, Carletta J. Group discussion as interactive dialogue or as serial monologue: The influence of group size. Psychological Science. 2000;**11**(6):481-486

[8] Hackman JR, Vidmar N. Effects of size and task type on group performance and member reactions. Sociometry. 1970;**33**(1):37-54. DOI: 10.2307/2786271

[9] Olson GM, Olson JS, Carter MR, Storrosten M. Small group design meetings: An analysis of collaboration. Human–Computer Interaction. 1992;**7**(4):347-374. DOI: 10.1207/s15327051hci0704_1

[10] Rosenberg L, Willcox G, Schumann H, Mani G. Towards collective superintelligence: Amplifying group IQ using conversational swarms. In: Proceedings of the 26th International Conference on Enterprise Information Systems. Vol. 1. ICEIS, SciTePress; 2024. pp. 759-766. DOI: 10.5220/0012687500003690. ISBN 978-989-758-692-7; ISSN 2184-4992

[11] Bénabou R. Groupthink: Collective delusions in organizations and markets. Review of Economic Studies. 2013;**80**(2):429-462

[12] Muchnik L, Aral S, Taylor SJ. Social influence bias: A randomized experiment. Science. 2013;**341**(6146): 647-651

[13] Lorenz J, Rauhut H, Schweitzer F, Helbing D. How social influence can undermine the wisdom of crowd effect. Proceedings of the National Academy of Sciences of the United States of America. 2011;**108**(22):9020-9025

[14] Ottaviani M, Sørensen PN. Aggregation of information and beliefs in prediction markets. In: London Conference on Information and Prediction Markets. Finance Research Unit; 2007

[15] Navajas J, Niella T, Garbulsky G, et al. Aggregated knowledge from a small number of debates outperforms the wisdom of large crowds. Nature Human Behaviour. 2018;**2**:126-132. DOI: 10.1038/s41562-017-0273-4

[16] Rosenberg L et al. Conversational swarms of humans and AI agents enable hybrid collaborative decision-making. In: 14th Annual Ubiquitous Computing, Electronics & Mobile Communication Conference (UEMCON 2024). 2024, October; New York, NY, USA.

[17] Rosenberg L, Willcox G, Schumann H. Conversational swarm intelligence (CSI) enables rapid group insights. In: 2023 IEEE 14th Annual Ubiquitous Computing, Electronics & Mobile Communication Conference (UEMCON), New York, NY, USA: IEEE; 2023. pp. 0534-0539. DOI: 10.1109/UEMCON59035.2023.10316130

[18] Rosenberg L, Willcox G, Schumann H, Mani G. Conversational swarm intelligence (CSI) enhances groupwise deliberation. In: 7th International Joint Conference on Advances in Computational Intelligence (IJCACI 2023; Oct 14, 2023). New Delhi;

[19] Krause J, Ruxton GD, Krause S. Swarm intelligence in animals and humans. Trends in Ecology & Evolution. 2010;**25**(1):28-34

[20] Seeley TD, Buhrman SC. Nest-site selection in honeybees: How well do swarms implement the 'best-of-N' decision rule? Behavioral Ecology and Sociobiology. 2001;**49**:416-427

[21] Seeley TD et al. Stop signals provide cross inhibition in collective decision-making by honeybee swarms. Science. 2012;**335**(6064):108-111

[22] Rosenberg L, Willcox G. Artificial swarm intelligence. In: Intelligent Systems and Applications: Proceedings of the 2019 Intelligent Systems Conference (IntelliSys). Vol. 1. Springer International Publishing; 2020. pp. 1054-1070

[23] Seeley TD. Honeybee Democracy. Princeton Univ. Press; 2010

[24] Seeley TD, Visscher PK. Choosing a home: How the scouts in a honey bee swarm perceive the completion of their group decision making. Behavioral Ecology and Sociobiology;**54**(5):511-520

[25] Rosenberg LB. Human swarming, a real-time method for parallel distributed intelligence. In: 2015 Swarm/Human Blended Intelligence Workshop (SHBI). IEEE; 2015. pp. 1-7. DOI: 10.1109/SHBI.2015.7321685

[26] Rosenberg L, Pescetelli N, Willcox G. Artificial swarm intelligence amplifies accuracy when predicting financial markets. In: 2017 IEEE 8th Annual Ubiquitous Computing, Electronics and Mobile Communication Conference (UEMCON). IEEE; 2017. pp. 58-62

[27] Patel BN, Rosenberg L, Willcox G, et al. Human–machine partnership with artificial intelligence for chest radiograph diagnosis. NPJ Digital Medicine. 2019;**2**:111. DOI: 10.1038/s41746-019-0189-7

[28] Rosenberg L, Lungren M, Halabi S, Willcox G, Baltaxe D, Lyons M. Artificial swarm intelligence employed to amplify diagnostic accuracy in radiology. In: 2018 IEEE 9th Annual Information Technology Electronics and Mobile Communication Conference (IEMCON). IEEE; 2018. pp. 1186-1191

[29] Askay D, Metcalf L, Rosenberg L, Willcox D. Enhancing group social perceptiveness through a swarm-based decision-making platform. In: Proceedings of 52nd Hawaii International Conference on System Sciences, HICSS-52. IEEE; 2019

[30] Rosenberg L, Willcox G, Askay D, Metcalf L, Harris E. Amplifying the social intelligence of teams through human swarming. In: 2018 First International Conference on Artificial

Intelligence for Industries (AI4I), Laguna Hills, CA, USA. 2018. pp. 23-26. DOI: 10.1109/AI4I.2018.8665698

[31] Willcox G, Rosenberg L, Burgman M, Marcoci A. Prioritizing policy objectives in polarized groups using artificial swarm intelligence. In: 2020 IEEE Conference on Cognitive and Computational Aspects of Situation Management (CogSIMA). Victoria, BC, Canada: IEEE; 2020. pp. 1-9. DOI: 10.1109/CogSIMA49017.2020.9216182

[32] Rosenberg L, Baltaxe D, Pescetelli N. Crowds vs swarms, a comparison of intelligence. In: 2016 Swarm/Human Blended Intelligence Workshop (SHBI). Cleveland, OH, USA: IEEE; 2016. pp. 1-4

[33] Rosenberg L, Willcox G. Artificial swarms find social optima. In: 2018 IEEE Conference on Cognitive and Computational Aspects of Situation Management (CogSIMA), Boston, MA, USA: IEEE; 2018. pp. 174-178. DOI: 10.1109/COGSIMA.2018.8423987

[34] Rosenberg L, Willcox G, Schumann H, Mani G. Conversational swarm intelligence amplifies the accuracy of networked groupwise deliberations. In: 2024 IEEE 14th Annual Computing and Communication Workshop and Conference (CCWC), Las Vegas, NV, USA: IEEE; 2024. pp. 0086-0091. DOI: 10.1109/CCWC60891.2024.10427807

[35] Parrish JK, Viscido S, Grünbaum D. Self-organized fish schools: An examination of emergent properties. Biological Bulletin. 2002;**202**(3):296-305

[36] Bronkhorst AW. The cocktail party phenomenon: A review on speech intelligibility in multiple-talker conditions. Acta Acustica United with Acustica. 2000;**86**:117-128 [Accessed: November 16, 2020]

[37] Rosenberg L, et al. Conversational swarm intelligence, a pilot study. arXiv.org. 2023. Available from: https://arxiv.org/abs/2309.03220

[38] US Patent 11,949,638. Methods and systems for hyperchat conversations among large networked populations with collective intelligence amplification

[39] Willcox G et al. Hyperswarms: A new architecture for amplifying collective intelligence. In: 2021 IEEE 12th Annual Information Technology, Electronics and Mobile Communication Conference (IEMCON). IEEE; 2021

[40] Graylin A, Rosenberg L. Our Next Reality. Nicholas Brealey Pub; 2024

[41] Rosenberg L, Schumann H, Dishop C, Willcox G, Woolley A, Mani G. Large-scale group brainstorming using conversational swarm intelligence (CSI) versus traditional chat. arXiv arXiv:2412.14205. 2024

[42] US Patent 12,231,383. Methods and systems for enabling collective superintelligence

[43] Marsh E, Vallejos EP, Spence A. Overloaded by information or worried about missing out on it: A quantitative study of stress, burnout, and mental health implications in the digital workplace. SAGE Open. 2024;**14**(3). DOI: 10.1177/21582440241268830

[44] Mark G, Gudith D, Klocke U. The cost of interrupted work: More speed and stress. In: Proceedings of the SIGCHI Conference on Human Factors in Computing Systems. 2008. pp. 107-110

[45] Thompson, C. Slack is Ruining Work, Wired. Available from: https://www.wired.com/story/slack-ruining-work

[46] Marsh E, Vallejos EP, Spence A. The digital workplace and its dark side: An

integrative review. Computers in Human Behavior. 2022;**128**:107118

[47] Montrief T, Haas MR, Gottlieb M, Siegal D, Chan T. Thinking outside the inbox: Use of slack in clinical groups as a collaborative team communication platform. AEM Education and Training. 2020;**5**(1):121

[48] USPTO US2025001612. Methods and systems for enabling large-scale conversational deliberations among human groups and AI-powered conversational agents. 2023. DOI: 10.13140/RG.2.2.23689.35686

[49] Willcox G et al. Validating a new collective intelligence Technology for Accurate Ranking Using Artificial Swarm Intelligence. In: Proceedings of the Future Technologies Conference. Cham: Springer Nature Switzerland; 2023. pp. 290-304

[50] Jaiswal A, Arun CJ, Varma A. Rebooting employees: Upskilling for artificial intelligence in multinational corporations. In: Artificial Intelligence and International HRM. Routledge; 2023. pp. 114-143

[51] Gabsi AEH. Integrating artificial intelligence in industry 4.0: Insights, challenges, and future prospects–A literature review. Annals of Operations Research. 2024:1-28

[52] Farrow E. Determining the human to AI workforce ratio–exploring future organizational scenarios and the implications for anticipatory workforce planning. Technology in Society. 2022;**68**:101879

[53] Rosenberg L. Keeping up with AI: Why humanity must cultivate a 'hive mind'. Futurism. 2016. Available from: https://futurism.com/keeping-humanity-must-cultivate-hive-mind

[54] Schemmer M, Hemmer P, Kühl N, Benz C, Satzger G. Should I follow AI-based advice? Measuring appropriate reliance in human-AI decision-making. arXiv preprint arXiv:2204.06916. 2022

[55] Rastogi C, Zhang Y, Wei D, Varshney KR, Dhurandhar A, Tomsett R. Deciding fast and slow: The role of cognitive biases in AI-assisted decision-making. Proceedings of the ACM on Human-Computer Interaction. 2022;**6**(CSCW1):1-22

[56] Rosenberg L. The manipulation problem: Conversational AI as a threat to epistemic agency. In: 2023 CHI Workshop on Generative AI and HCI (GenAICHI 2023). ACM; 2023. DOI: 10.48550/arXiv.2306.11748

[57] Rosenberg L. Generative AI as a dangerous new form of media. In: Proceedings of the 17th International Multi-Conference on Society, Cybernetics and Informatics (IMSCI 2023). 2023. DOI: 10.54808/IMSCI2023.01.165

Chapter 5

Decision Science for Carbon Emission Reduction: Integrating Systemic Frameworks and Emerging Technologies

Chang-Jing Ji, Xiaodan Wang and Xiang-Yu Wang

Abstract

Climate change represents one of the most complex, multi-scale decision-making challenges of the twenty-first century, demanding interdisciplinary approaches to balance scientific uncertainty, socioeconomic equity, and long-term sustainability. Traditional policy frameworks often fail to address the dynamic interdependencies between climate systems, natural resources, ecological environment, human behavior, and technological innovation. This chapter positions climate change decision-making within the broader discipline of decision science, emphasizing its unique need for hybrid methodologies that integrate predictive analytics, behavioral insights, and ethical considerations under deep uncertainty. We will first define and discuss the complexities of carbon reduction decisions and position decision science as the linchpin for achieving a net-zero future. Secondly, summarize the foundational theories and quantitative tools in carbon reduction-making. Thirdly, challenges and future directions are proposed to identify frontiers in carbon reduction decision science. By bridging foundational theories with emerging computational tools, this chapter aims to advance the development of climate decision.

Keywords: climate decision-making, carbon emission reduction, integrated assessment models, computable general equilibrium models, uncertainty analysis

1. Introduction

Climate change represents one of the most pressing global challenges of our time. The Sixth Assessment Report from the Intergovernmental Panel on Climate Change (IPCC) reveals that atmospheric carbon dioxide concentrations have surged to 410 ppm, a level not seen in nearly 2 million years. Furthermore, the global average surface temperature has escalated by approximately 1.1°C since the baseline of the pre-industrial revolution (1850–1900), with the rate of temperature rise over the past half-century surpassing any similar period in the preceding two millennia [1]. The impacts of climate change are widespread and far-reaching, affecting both the natural environment and human society. On the environmental side, climate change leads to glacier melting, sea level rise, more frequent and severe meteorological events (such as floods and droughts), reduced agricultural productivity, loss of biodiversity, and changes in ecosystems. For societal systems, climate change poses huge negative impacts on health, urban management, and infrastructure. Simultaneously, the interaction of climatic factors is escalating in complexity, leading to the potential for concurrent disasters, thereby complicating our response [2]. According to the IPCC report, there is a 50% probability that global warming will exceed 1.5°C in the ensuing 20 years. Surpassing this threshold may precipitate more severe and irreversible impacts, including rising sea levels, ecosystem degradation, water shortages, species extinction, increased frequency of extreme events, and the spread of diseases, all of which will significantly impact human survival and development [2].

Addressing climate change is of paramount importance, necessitating a robust international response. The United Nations Framework Convention on Climate Change (UNFCCC) of 1992 established an international legal framework for cooperative efforts in addressing climate change, and it also clarified the principle of "common but differentiated responsibilities." The Third Conference of the Parties to the UNFCCC in 1997 adopted the first legally binding climate agreement, the "Kyoto Protocol," which set binding emission reduction targets for major developed countries and three cooperative emission reduction mechanisms. The twenty-first Conference of the Parties to the UNFCCC in 2015 adopted the "Paris Agreement," which required countries to participate in global emission reduction through a bottom-up "National Determined Contribution" (NDC) approach, and further to maintain the global average temperature increase below 2°C by 2100 and to pursue efforts to limit the temperature increase to within 1.5°C.

However, it is a long-term and multifaceted task for addressing climate change, as it has evolved to encompass political, economic, environmental, and ethical dimensions, making the achievement of emission reduction targets challenging. Politically, a significant disparity exists in emission reduction responsibilities between developed and developing nations. The rapid expansion of new energy industries has heightened resistance from traditional energy sector interest groups. Economically, combating climate change necessitates substantial investments in emission reduction technology research, energy infrastructure modifications, and industrial advancements. This necessitates a delicate balance between economic progression and emission reduction objectives. Furthermore, the commitments of developed nations to provide climate investment and financing for developing nations present challenges in terms of fund scale, distribution, and utilization. Environmentally, climate change has intensified problems such as pollution, water contamination, frequent severe weather events, and imbalanced biodiversity. Ethically, the consequences of climate change are both prolonged and unpredictable. Addressing the ethical dilemmas arising from the need to meet the requirements of both current and future generations, while simultaneously ensuring a sustainable ecological environment for posterity, is of utmost importance. Moreover, the issue of equitable global responsibility and resource distribution, especially when taking into account the developmental rights and interests of developing countries, represents another crucial ethical conundrum within the framework of climate change. Striking a balance among economic growth, environmental conservation, political viability, and ethical principles within the predefined emission reduction targets remains a formidable challenge in our emission reduction decision-making procedures.

Scientific and rational emission reduction decisions are an important means to address climate change. An increasing number of studies incorporate climate, economy, energy, and environment into a unified analytical framework, taking into account the long-term, complexity, uncertainty, and regional imbalances of climate change [3–6]. They employ tools such as multi-objective programming, scenario analysis, and machine learning to conduct climate emission reduction decision-making and evaluation. Therefore, this chapter focuses on the analytical framework and cutting-edge technologies for carbon emission reduction decisions, systematically reviewing the application of decision science in the field of carbon emission reduction.

2. Foundational theories of carbon emission reduction decisions

Carbon emission reduction decisions mainly revolve around how much to reduce, when to reduce, and how to reduce [7]. The question of how much to reduce essentially involves determining how much carbon dioxide can still be emitted under the constraints of temperature control targets. At the global level, the total amount of reduction or emission constraints needs to be clarified based on global temperature control targets. Within individual countries or industries, the total global reduction amount must be distributed in accordance with global reduction targets, integrated with their own. Consequently, several theoretical principles for the allocation of emission responsibilities have been developed, including the principles of common but differentiated responsibility, fairness, and efficiency [8]. The timing of emission reductions is primarily predicated on the theory of intergenerational equity, which considers how to balance the responsibilities and benefits of both contemporary and future generations to achieve global optimization [9]. The question of how to reduce emissions not only pertains to the choice of reduction mechanisms but also to the uncertainty of emission reduction technologies [5], essentially requiring a balance between the costs and benefits of emission reduction. The subsequent text will delve into the theoretical underpinnings of carbon emission reduction decisions.

2.1 The principles of emission reduction responsibility-sharing

The principle of fairness refers to the obligation of countries to undertake emission reductions that match their capabilities and responsibilities based on their own economic, social, and historical emission factors in addressing climate change [3]. This principle emphasizes the rationality and fairness of responsibility allocation, avoiding excessive burdens on some countries due to unfair responsibility allocation, while others evade their responsibilities. The principle of Common but Differentiated Responsibilities and Respective Capabilities (CBDR-RC) is a core principle in the UNFCCC. It emphasizes that countries have a common responsibility to address climate change, but due to differences in development levels, historical emissions, and economic capabilities, they should undertake different responsibilities and obligations [10]. The principle of efficiency mainly refers to the allocation of emission rights, aiming to ensure the most rational use of resources to achieve the maximization of societal welfare. It emphasizes that under the constraints of limited environmental capacity, emission rights should be allocated to entities that can reduce pollution at the lowest cost or those that can create the maximum economic value through the rational use of emission rights [8].

The current Paris Agreement adopts a bottom-up approach to determining emission reduction responsibilities. Therefore, a significant challenge it faces is how to integrate global emission reduction pressures with the responsibility sharing among countries to ensure that the autonomous contribution targets proposed by countries align with global temperature control objectives. This requires us to balance the overall with the local when allocating emission reduction responsibilities. Under the constraints of global temperature control objectives, we aim for the maximization of total regional welfare to address the issue of regional responsibility allocation for carbon emission reduction.

2.2 The theory of intergenerational equity

The theory of intergenerational equity highlights the necessity of safeguarding the interests of future generations, alongside those of the present generation, in resource allocation and environmental management. The core of the intergenerational equity theory is to ensure the sustainability of resources and the environment so that future generations can enjoy similar resources and quality of life as contemporary people. The Paris Agreement is an important embodiment of the theory of intergenerational equity in international climate governance. The agreement requires countries to undertake their emission reduction responsibilities according to their own capabilities, and to provide financial and technical support for developing countries, so as to ensure that the global temperature increase is controlled within 2°C and efforts are made to limit the temperature increase to 1.5°C. This is not only for the interests of contemporary people but also for the survival and development of future generations.

It requires us to construct an intertemporal equilibrium model in the decision-making process of emission reductions, to achieve the maximization of intertemporal welfare under given constraints. In addition, the discount rate is a key parameter for measuring intergenerational equity. Choosing a lower discount rate can better reflect the responsibility toward future generations, promoting the realization of intergenerational fairness [11]. This makes the losses caused by future climate change when discounted to the present, quite significant, thus necessitating substantial emissions reductions now. Meanwhile, some scholars advocate for determining the discount rate based on the real return rates of consumer behavior and capital in the market (using either the producer interest rate or the consumer interest rate), aiming to maximize social resources [12, 13]. The discount rates derived from this approach are relatively higher, leading to a slower reduction in emissions. Thus, it is important to coordinate the costs of current climate change mitigation and the losses brought about by future climate change and balance long-term and short-term emission reductions, when setting a positive but not aggressive welfare discount rate, comprehensively.

2.3 Theoretical comparative analysis of quantity-based and price-based mechanisms

An effective carbon emission reduction mechanism is an important way to achieve carbon emission reduction targets, and carbon pricing policies are effective tools to achieve emission reduction targets at a lower cost. By pricing carbon emissions, carbon pricing policies incorporate the negative externality costs caused by emitters into their actual costs, prompting them to make optimal production decisions [14]. Carbon pricing policies mainly include two types: carbon tax and carbon emission trading. The carbon tax is a price-based tool originating from Pigou's tax [15], which levies a fixed rate on each ton of carbon dioxide emissions but does not set an emission ceiling, thus the reduction is uncertain; carbon trading is a quantity-based tool originating from Coase's theorem [16], which sets an emission ceiling, but the carbon price is endogenously determined by the carbon market, thus the price is uncertain.

The debate between carbon trading and carbon tax has been long-standing. In a market environment with complete information, decision-makers can achieve the same outcomes using either price control (carbon tax) or quantity control (carbon emissions trading) when the marginal benefit from abatement equals the marginal cost. However, these two policies significantly diverge in practice, particularly in terms of operational costs, political risks, and emission reduction effects. Each carries its own set of advantages, making it challenging for policymakers to choose. Furthermore, factors such as information asymmetry, limitations in technological evaluations, and unpredictable future climate changes contribute to the strong uncertainty in estimating the marginal benefit from abatement and the marginal cost [17, 18].

In response to these uncertainties, a price-quantity comparative analysis examines the performance of two carbon emission reduction measures under uncertainty at the theoretical level, providing valuable references for both decision-makers and researchers. Among them, the decision-making method proposed by Weitzman [11], which compares marginal costs and marginal benefit slopes—known as the Relative Slope Decision-making Criterion (RSDC)—has been widely applied and has had the most profound impact. The key of RSDC is to analyze the slopes of marginal cost and marginal benefit curves, which essentially further compares the sensitivity of cost and benefit changes to welfare, and reduces the uncertainty of results by controlling the side with higher sensitivity.

Weitzman set up a variable Δ to represent the difference between price control welfare W(p) and quantity control welfare W(q) and conducted a static analysis of the economic properties of cost and benefit functions, deriving formula (1).

$$\Delta = W(p) - W(q) = \frac{\sigma^2}{2C''^2}(B'' + C'') \tag{1}$$

Where σ^2 represents the variance of marginal abatement cost; C'' ($C'' > 0$) represents the slope of the marginal abatement cost; B'' ($B'' < 0$) represents the slope of the marginal benefit. When $|C''| > |B''|$, $\Delta > 0$, price-based mechanism is more cost-effective than quantity-based mechanism; otherwise, quantity-based mechanism is more cost-effective.

The framework of RSDC provides a theoretical method for the selection of market emission reduction mechanisms under uncertain conditions. Scholars can estimate the marginal abatement costs and marginal benefits through climate change comprehensive assessment models or computable general equilibrium models and further fit the marginal abatement cost curve and marginal benefit curve. Then, using formula (1), they can select the optimal market emission reduction tool to answer the question of how to reduce emissions from a policy perspective.

2.4 Game-theoretic models for international cooperation

The Paris Agreement establishes a bottom-up voluntary emission reduction rule based on common responsibility to deal with how much emission reductions by each country, but countries face a public goods game on carbon emission reduction. Every country has the incentive to reduce carbon emissions, but at the same time, it will also consider the emission reduction efforts of other countries, trying to benefit from them without paying too much cost. Public goods have the characteristics of non-exclusion and non-rivalry, that is, one person's consumption of the good does not reduce the consumption of others, and it is impossible to prevent others from consuming the good. This feature leads to the "free-rider" problem, where individuals may tend to not contribute resources and hope to benefit from the contributions of others [19, 20].

Game theory has been widely used in the "free-rider" problem. Game theory is the study of the decisions and decision-making equilibrium issues when the behaviors of decision-making entities directly interact with each other. The behavioral strategies of decision-making entities in game theory mainly include "cooperation" and "non-cooperation" [21]. The key to conducting global emissions reduction strategy analysis lies in the game and balance of decision-making behaviors between countries adopting "cooperative" or "non-cooperative" strategies. This forms "equilibrium" or "non-equilibrium" game situations at different development stages, thereby achieving the maximum carbon emissions reduction effect. Cooperative game theory emphasizes that countries should jointly address climate change through negotiation and cooperation to achieve global emissions reduction goals and common interests. Noncooperative game theory, on the other hand, emphasizes that countries may take independent actions, and even to a certain extent ignore the need for global cooperation, in the process of maximizing their own interests.

Cooperative and noncooperative games have been used in practical climate change modeling. In the modeling of cooperative games, the maximization of global social welfare is mostly set as the objective function, and the global social welfare is the weighted sum of the discounted values of regional welfare, as shown in Eq. (2):

Max:

$$W = \sum_{i=1} \int_{0}^{T} \theta_i U_i e^{-\delta t} dt \tag{2}$$

Where W is social welfare, θ_i is weight of welfare in region i, t is time, δ is discount rate (time preference rate), U_i is regional utility (or the economic well-being), for the Dynamic Integrated Climate-Economy (DICE) model, the utility is associated with a path of consumption [22]. Each region first determines the social welfare weight, then decides its own emission reduction rate, and finally, the greenhouse gas emissions from all regions are summed to obtain the total emissions for the whole society. In cooperative games, regions strive to maximize their respective social welfare weights; the larger the weight, the less responsibility a region bears for emissions reduction, and the greater the benefits it receives from other regions' emission reductions. The most prevalent method of weight-setting assumes equal marginal welfare for each region, emphasizing fairness. However, this equal-weighted cooperative emission reduction approach can potentially cause welfare losses in certain regions, leading to instability in global cooperative emission reduction. Yang proposed a second-best optimal cooperative Lindahl weight that enhances the welfare of each region compared to noncooperative emission reduction, thereby establishing a stable global cooperative emission reduction mechanism [23].

In the modeling of noncooperative game scenarios, countries only consider their own interests in emission reduction. The target function is set as the maximization of the social welfare in a single region, as shown in Eq. (3):

Max:

$$W_i = \int_0^T \theta_i U_i e^{-\delta t} dt \tag{3}$$

Where each region pursues the maximization of its own welfare under the condition of given emission reduction paths of other regions. After completing multi-region optimization, a Nash equilibrium is achieved in the noncooperative game scenario, at which point no region can obtain more welfare by adjusting its own emission reduction strategy. The emission reduction effect of noncooperative game is poor, which fails to control the temperature target and may cause a greater risk of climate loss for future generations.

Generally, game-theoretic models often combine with multi-region or multi-agent integrated assessment models to answer how much emissions should be reduced at a country level. Thus, Eqs. (2) and (3) are usually set as object functions in the integrated assessment models.

3. Quantitative tools in carbon reduction-making

Carbon emission reduction decisions rely on scientifically effective quantitative methods. Response to the key scientific issues of carbon emission reduction decisions, it is required to systematically answer questions such as how much to reduce, when to reduce, and how to reduce. In order to achieve cost-effective emission reductions, numerous studies have developed systematic assessment tools for quantitative analysis, integrating economic, energy, environmental, and climate issues into a unified analytical framework. By using dynamic optimization methods, the optimal allocation of emission reduction actions between regions and industries is achieved, balancing the costs and benefits of intertemporal emission reductions, and seeking the optimal path for emission reduction. This chapter will focus on the comprehensive assessment models widely used in scientific research and IPCC reports, including integrated assessment model, computable general equilibrium model, and some advanced technologies.

3.1 Climate change integrated assessment model (IAM)

The climate change integrated assessment model serves as a critical tool in addressing research related to climate change. Its origins can be traced back to the 1960s, during a period of intense global environmental problem research in the twentieth century. The resolution of such problems necessitates insights from a broad array of disciplines, spanning from the natural sciences to the humanities and social sciences. These insights must be meticulously integrated to elucidate the fundamental structure of these problems and potential solutions [24]. Consequently, the "integrated assessment" policy evaluation process was initiated, leading to the development of interdisciplinary, large-scale simulation models. These models subsequently became central tools in the integrated assessment process, paving the way for the creation of the integrated assessment model [25]. William Nordhaus, in his seminal work published in 1991, integrated climate change into long-term macroeconomic analysis, thus establishing the roots of the climate change integrated assessment model [26]. His seminal contributions to this field were recognized when he was awarded the Nobel Prize in Economics.

IAMs bring together a number of steps from economic growth, through emissions and climate change, to the impact on the economy, and finally to the expected impact of climate policy (**Figure 1**). A general IAM consists of three basic modules coupled together [27]: the carbon cycle module (carbon emissions in **Figure 1**), the climate module (climate impact and damages in **Figure 1**), and the economic growth module (economic growth in **Figure 1**). In addition, an increasing number of models are establishing connections not only between economic, energy, and climate systems but also incorporating elements such as land, water, and extreme weather [25, 28]. IAMs can be divided into two categories, the Detailed Process Integrated Assessment Models (DP-IAMs) and the Benefit-Cost Integrated Assessment Model (BC-IAMs), according to the content covered, the complexity, and the level of detail in describing the climate-economic relationship [28].

BC-IAMs combine the mitigation costs and the sectoral impacts of climate change into a single economic indicator, such as GDP. Most BC-IAMs are optimization models, and are widely used to determine the optimal emission reduction path. Representative BC-IAMs include the Dynamic Integrated Climate-Economy Model (DICE) [27], the Regional Integrated Climate-Economy Model (RICE) [29], the Policy Analysis of the Greenhouse Effect (PAGE) [30], and the climate Framework for Uncertainty, Negotiation, and Distribution (FUND) [31]. The objective function of these models usually follows formulas (2) and (3).

The DP-IAMs seek to estimate climate change impacts at a detailed regional and sectoral level, with a focus on intra- and inter-sectoral interactions. It produces not only economic estimates of the impacts of climate change but also projections of the physical impacts of climate change, e.g., on reduced crop growth and land inundated by rising sea levels, providing more detailed policy guidance. The majority of DP-IAMs are either general or partial equilibrium models. They are characterized by a large number of parameters, intricate structures, and increased uncertainty, all of which complicate the process of monetizing the impacts of climate change. These models often focus on specific sectors or industries, including those related to agriculture, energy services, labor productivity, and coastal resources. Additionally, they assess nonmarket impacts

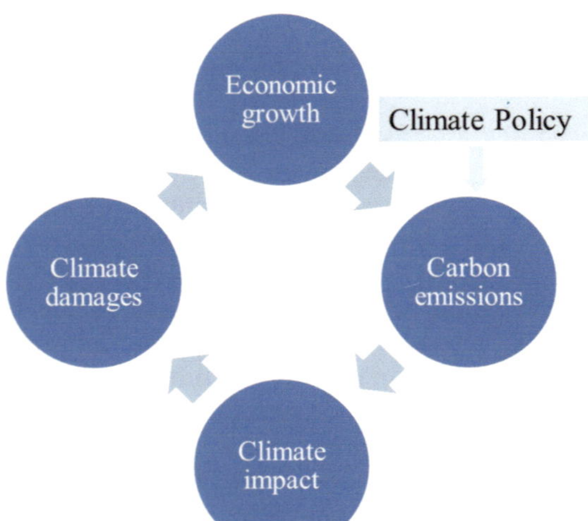

Figure 1.
Schematic of the IAM.

such as human health, mortality effects, and ecosystem effects. Many representative models are widely used, such as the Integrated Model to Assess the Greenhouse Effect (IMAGE) [32] and the Global Change Assessment Model (GCAM) [33].

3.2 Computable general equilibrium (CGE) model

Computable General Equilibrium (CGE) models delineate the intricate relationships among various economic sectors, entities, production factors (such as labor, capital, land, and resources), goods, and services across diverse regional scales (**Figure 2**). These models are adept at evaluating the impacts of climate change on production, consumption, endowment markets such as the labor and capital markets, and nonmarket effects, including those on human health risks, such as mortality effects, and ecosystems [34–36]. The majority of CGE models are augmented with satellite accounts, which encompass data on land use, crops, forestry, energy, and air pollution, to facilitate a comprehensive assessment of climate impacts [37–39]. It is imperative to note that while the CGE model itself is not inherently an optimization model, its formulation typically implies the optimal behavior of micro-subjects, such as maximizing residents' welfare and corporeal profits [39].

CGE models are paired to a climate module to evaluate the climate change impacts [40] either through a one-way connection, with fixed damage functions translating the biophysical impact of climate change into economic impact [41, 42], or a two-way connection, in which climate conditions and socioeconomic systems interact with each other. More specifically, (1) the CGE model predicts greenhouse gas (GHG) emissions based on projected future socioeconomic scenarios, (2) the climate module translates these emissions into concentrations and temperature changes, and finally, (3) climate damage functions simulate impacts of the climate condition into exogenous shocks, such as changes in productivity, endowments, production, and consumption patterns, to be fed back into the CGE model [43, 44]. Some representative models are widely used in climate change assessment, such as Emissions

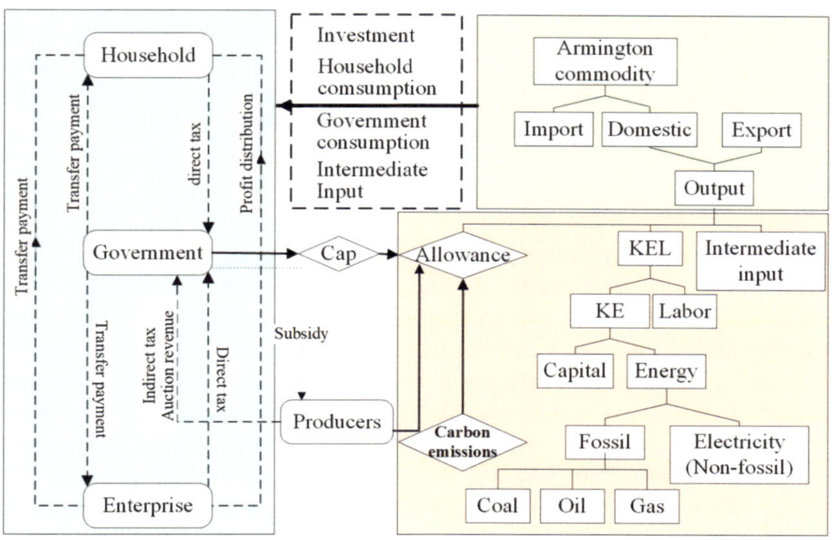

Figure 2.
Schematic of the CGE.

Prediction and Policy Analysis Model (EEPA) [45], Asia-Pacific Integrated Model/ Computable General Equilibrium (AIM/CGE) [46], and Global Trade Analysis Project-Energy (GTAP-E) [47].

3.3 Artificial intelligence (AI) or machine learning (ML) helps climate decisions

3.3.1 Scenario discovery

Climate decisions hinge on extensive data that encapsulates both climate projections and the evolution of human activities. This data spans a multitude of sources and modalities, including meteorology, geography, and economics. To ensure both traceability and comprehensiveness in developing new scenarios, it is imperative to commence with a thorough review of a vast array of scenario literature. This review aids in identifying and quantifying the key driving factors that will influence future developments [48]. AI/ML can be instrumental in managing such big data. These technologies can discern key driving factors across various systems, including social, earth, economic, and ecological, and subsequently generate future scenarios based on permutations and combinations of these different driving factors. Several AI/ML methods have already been employed for scenario discovery, including classification and regression trees [49], the patient rule induction method [50], and support vector classification [51].

3.3.2 Extreme events prediction

The precision of extreme climate prediction has significant implications for climate mitigation and adaptation strategies. However, predicting extreme events presents unique challenges, including the development of accurate predictive models from noisy, heterogeneous data with small sample sizes and limited annotations. AL/ML can effectively process large volumes of historical climate data and satellite images to identify early warning signals of extreme weather events, such as hurricanes, tornadoes, and droughts, thereby enhancing the accuracy of extreme climate prediction. Deep learning-based prediction techniques have gained prominence due to their capacity to handle large data volumes, capture complex nonlinear relationships, and reduce the need for manual feature engineering [52]. AI techniques such as Long Short-Term Memory (LSTM) [53], Support Vector Machine (SVM) models, and Convolutional Neural Networks (CNN) [54] can be integrated within climate models to improve predictions.

3.3.3 Model parameters and performance optimization

Model parameter uncertainty impacts both the precision and accuracy of climate models and escalates the risk in climate decision-making. This has ramifications for policy creation, public perception, and international cooperation. The integration of traditional integrated assessment models with advanced Artificial Intelligence/ machine learning technologies can lead to model enhancements and quantification of uncertainties. This process significantly mitigates the effect of parameter uncertainty on climate decisions, thereby boosting the scientific validity and effectiveness of climate decision-making. For example, the use of Bayesian neural networks [55] and Monte Carlo simulations [56] allows for the quantification of uncertainty in climate decision outcomes under potential parameters. The precision and reliability of model parameters can be bolstered through techniques such as cross-validation (Cross-validation), quantile mapping (Quantile Mapping), and deep learning [57, 58].

3.4 Comparison between different models

We compare the well-known models in **Table 1**. Generally, all models include carbon emissions and economic-related modules and can provide optimal economic development path, carbon emissions path, as well as carbon price path, from a global assessment or regional assessment. In addition, CB-IAMs are optimization models, while DB-IAMs and CGE models are partial/general equilibrium models as they provide more regional, sectoral, and industrial details.

Specifically, for CB-IAMs (such as DICE, PAGE), by balancing the costs of emission reduction actions and the climate losses avoided by reduction, the optimal emission reduction path and policy formulation can be determined, highlighting key issues such as discount rates and losses. However, CB-IAMs are unable to assess the indirect and interactive effects between climate change and economy. Moreover, when the impacts of industries and regions are aggregated into a single economic indicator, it may lead to the form of the damage function and key parameters greatly influencing the choice of emission reduction strategies, such as in the calculation of social carbon costs under different loss functions, where the discrepancies are too large [25]. For DP-IAMs (such as GCAM and IMAGE), they consider physical and economic interactions between influencing sectors and their feedback to the climate system, seek to provide predictions of climate change impacts at detailed regional and sectoral levels, offering more specific policy guidance. Furthermore, DP-IAMs can be adjusted and expanded according to different research needs, applicable to various policy assessments and research scenarios. Due to the detailed process simulation and multidisciplinary integration of the DP-IAMs, its structure is relatively complex, with high computational costs and requirements for data and parameters, and the predictive results exhibit significant uncertainty. The CGE model (such as EPPA, AIM/CGE) fundamentally hinges on the optimization behaviors of economic entities. It employs the correlation between macro and micro variables as a connecting bridge and considers the entire economic system as its subject of analysis. It can describe the interactions between multiple markets and their participating entities. Compared to the IAMs, CGE models have the advantage of being able to analyze direct economic effects of climate shocks and the way in which they propagate across sectors through price changes and substitution effects while being able to consider adaptation

Model	Type	Module	Software
DICE	Welfare maximization	Carbon cycle, climate, and economic growth	GAMS
PAGE	Welfare maximization	Carbon cycle, climate, and sea level rise module and economic growth module	Julia/R
GCAM	Partial equilibrium	Climate, economy, energy, land, and water	R
IMAGE	Partial equilibrium	Emission, concentration, climate, sea level rise, and socioeconomic impact	Dynamo
EPPA	General equilibrium	Environment, energy, economy, land use, and resource	GAMS
AIM/CGE	General equilibrium	Emission, air pollution, economy, land	GAMS

Table 1.
Comparisons between different models.

responses from producers and consumers. Nevertheless, CGE models are not without their limitations. They necessitate a substantial amount of input data and economic parameters. Additionally, computational complexities emerge during the resolution of optimization problems characterized by high spatial and temporal dimensionality.

4. Future perspectives

Decisions regarding climate emission reductions form the crux of global responses to climate change; however, their complexity, multi-scale nature, and conflicts of interest present substantial challenges. There remain unresolved issues in the extant research within this field. This paper puts forth the following potential directions for future research:

1. Second-best climate policy. The pursuit of a second-best climate policy has gained realism due to the challenges associated with implementing unified carbon pricing and the high uncertainty of estimating social carbon costs [59, 60]. Future research should delve into issues such as imperfect markets, technological constraints, and barriers to international cooperation. Moreover, the game of climate policy is an intricate and multidimensional issue that spans multiple levels at international, domestic, and industry scales. At present, there is a paucity of studies on climate games, with most analyses focusing on the extreme situations of cooperative and noncooperative games between countries, which are often difficult to implement in practice. Thus, creating an urgent need for analysis of frontier issues such as the second-best equilibrium based on game theory.

2. Cutting-edge climate mitigation technologies. The prompt achievement of carbon neutrality *via* innovation and large-scale implementation of these technologies is the core underpinning for attaining net-zero emission targets. It is imperative to conduct an exhaustive assessment of these technologies to address the pressing challenges associated with global climate change and advancing sustainable development. However, the choice of technological paths may likely trigger cross-system risks to natural and socioeconomic systems in the short term [61]. Cutting-edge climate mitigation technologies encompass conventional efforts that utilize decarbonization techniques to minimize CO_2 emissions. These include renewable energy sources, fuel switching, efficiency enhancements, nuclear power, and carbon capture, storage, and utilization. Additionally, they comprise negative emissions technologies and geoengineering methods [62]. Notably, most existing comprehensive assessment models for climate decisions do not systematically integrate these cutting-edge technologies into a unified framework, thereby neglecting a thorough analysis of the risks and benefits associated with various emission reduction pathways.

3. Uncertainty Analysis. Due to various factors such as information asymmetry, unpredictable technological advancements, unpredictable future climate changes, and the difficulty of policy implementation, the estimation of emission reduction costs and benefits has strong uncertainty, which also poses challenges to climate reduction decision-making [63, 64]. Existing research mainly uses probabilities to quantify uncertainty, such as Bayesian and Monte Carlo simulation methods [5]; however, due to limitations such as computational complexity and data dependency, it can only carry out uncertainty analysis for key parameters.

In the future, tools such as deep learning can be used to assess multidimensional uncertainties such as technological advancements, economic development, loss functions, and extreme climates.

5. Conclusions

Climate change represents one of the most complex, multi-scale decision-making challenges of the twenty-first century. In this paper, we provide a theoretical analysis framework for carbon emission reduction decisions, elaborating on key issues and theoretical methods in the field of carbon emission reduction decision-making from four dimensions: allocation of emission reduction, timing of emission reduction, choice of emission reduction mechanisms, and game of emission reduction entities. It then introduces mainstream tools for quantitative macro carbon emission reduction decisions, including IAMs, CGE models, and AI/ML models. Finally, it proposes that future research on carbon emission reduction decisions can further focus on optimal/second-best climate policies, comprehensive assessment of cutting-edge climate mitigation technologies, and uncertainty analysis.

Acknowledgements

This study is supported by the National Natural Science Foundation of China, No. 72404186; and Chenguang Program of Shanghai Education Development Foundation and Shanghai Municipal Education Commission; and Shanghai Pujiang Program, No. 24PJA083.

Conflict of interest

The authors declare no conflict of interest.

Author details

Chang-Jing Ji[1*], Xiaodan Wang[1*] and Xiang-Yu Wang[2]

1 Institute of Carbon Neutrality, ShanghaiTech University, Shanghai, China

2 Environmental Development Center of the Ministry of Ecology and Environment, Beijing, China

*Address all correspondence to: jichj@shanghaitech.edu.cn; wangxd2@shanghaitech.edu.cn

References

[1] Masson-Delmotte V, Zhai P, Pirani A, et al. Climate change 2021: The physical science basis. In: Contribution of Working Group I to the Sixth Assessment Report of the Intergovernmental Panel on Climate Change. Cambridge: Cambridge University Press; 2022

[2] IPCC. Climate Change 2022: Impacts, Adaptation and Vulnerability. Cambridge: Cambridge University Press; 2022

[3] Yu B, Zhao Z, Wei YM, et al. Approaching national climate targets in China considering the challenge of regional inequality. Nature Communications. 2023;**14**(1):8342

[4] Roelfsema M, van Soest HL, Harmsen M, et al. Taking stock of national climate policies to evaluate implementation of the Paris Agreement. Nature Communications. 2020;**11**(1):2096

[5] Zhang S, Chen W. Assessing the energy transition in China towards carbon neutrality with a probabilistic framework. Nature Communications. 2022;**13**(1):87

[6] Morfeldt J, Larsson J, Andersson D, et al. Emission pathways and mitigation options for achieving consumption-based climate targets in Sweden. Communications Earth & Environment. 2023;**4**(1):342

[7] Wei Y, Chen W. The carbon mitigation "time-space-efficiency-benefit"(TSEB) coordination theory: Overall framework. Journal of Beijing Institute of Technology (Social Sciences Edition). 2024;**26**(5):1-11

[8] Wei YM, Wang L, Liao H, et al. Responsibility accounting in carbon allocation: A global perspective. Applied Energy. 2014;**130**:122-133

[9] Alvarez-Cuadrado F, Van Long N. A mixed Bentham–Rawls criterion for intergenerational equity: Theory and implications. Journal of Environmental Economics and Management. 2009;**58**(2):154-168

[10] Rajamani L. The principle of common but differentiated responsibilities and respective capabilities in the international climate change regime. In: Research Handbook on Climate Disaster Law. Cheltenham: Edward Elgar Publishing; 2018. pp. 46-60

[11] Weitzman ML. Prices vs. quantities. The Review of Economic Studies. 1974;**41**(4):477-491

[12] Nordhaus WD. A review of the stern review on the economics of climate change. Journal of Economic Literature. 2007;**45**(3):686-702

[13] Newell RG, Pizer WA. Uncertain discount rates in climate policy analysis. Energy Policy. 2004;**32**(4):519-529

[14] Montgomery WD. Markets in licenses and efficient pollution control programs. Journal of Economic Theory. 1972;**5**(3):395-418

[15] Nordhaus WD. To tax or not to tax: Alternative approaches to slowing global warming. Review of Environmental Economics and Policy. 2007;**1**(1):26-44

[16] Coase RH. The problem of social cost. Journal of Law & Economics. 1960;**56**(4):837-877

[17] Adar Z, Griffin JM. Uncertainty and the choice of pollution control

instruments. Journal of Environmental Economics and Management. 1976;**3**(3):178-188

[18] Fishelson G. Emission control policies under uncertainty. Journal of Environmental Economics and Management. 1976;**3**(3):189-197

[19] Hoel M. Efficient climate policy in the presence of free riders. Journal of Environmental Economics and Management. 1994;**27**(3):259-274

[20] Yang Z. The Environment and Externality: Theory, Algorithms and Applications. Cambridge: Cambridge University Press; 2020

[21] Hillebrand E, Hillebrand M. Win as a Team or Fail as Individuals: Cooperation and Non-Cooperation in the Climate Tax Game. Freiburg im Breisgau: University of Freiburg Working paper; 2023

[22] Barrage L, Nordhaus W. Policies, projections, and the social cost of carbon: Results from the DICE-2023 model. Proceedings of the National Academy of Sciences. 2024;**121**(13):e2312030121

[23] Yang Z. Strategic Bargaining and Cooperation in Greenhouse Gas Mitigations: An Integrated Assessment Modeling Approach. Cambridge, MA: MIT Press; 2008

[24] Hornsey MJ, Harris EA, Bain PG, et al. Meta-analyses of the determinants and outcomes of belief in climate change. Nature Climate Change. 2016;**6**(6):622-626

[25] Weyant J, Davidson O, Dowlatabadi H, et al. Integrated assessment of climate change: An overview and comparison of approaches and results. In: Climate change 1995: Economic and social dimensions of climate change. Cambridge: Cambridge University Press; 1996

[26] Nordhaus WD. To slow or not to slow: The economics of the greenhouse effect. The Economic Journal. 1991;**101**(407):920-937

[27] Nordhaus W. Projections and uncertainties about climate change in an era of minimal climate policies. American Economic Journal: Economic Policy. 2018;**10**(3):333-360

[28] Weyant J. Some contributions of integrated assessment models of global climate change. Review of Environmental Economics and Policy. 2017;**11**(1):115-137

[29] Nordhaus WD, Yang Z. A regional dynamic general-equilibrium model of alternative climate-change strategies. The American Economic Review. 1996;**86**:741-765

[30] Moore FC, Rising J, Lollo N, et al. Mimi-PAGE, an open-source implementation of the PAGE09 integrated assessment model. Scientific Data. 2018;**5**(1):1-8

[31] Anthoff D, Tol RSJ. The uncertainty about the social cost of carbon: A decomposition analysis using fund. Climatic Change. 2013;**117**:515-530

[32] Rotmans J, De Boois H, Swart RJ. An integrated model for the assessment of the greenhouse effect: The Dutch approach. Climatic Change. 1990;**16**:331-356

[33] Edmonds JA, Wise MA, MacCracken CN. Advanced Energy Technologies and Climate Change an Analysis Using the Global Change Assessment Model (GCAM). Richland, WA (United States): Pacific Northwest National Laboratory (PNNL); 1994

[34] Raviv O, Palatnik RR, Castellini M, et al. Synergies of CGE and IAM modelling for climate change implications on WEFE nexus in the Mediterranean. Climate Risk Management. 2024;**44**:100608

[35] Tang BJ, Ji CJ, Hu YJ, et al. Optimal carbon allowance price in China's carbon emission trading system: Perspective from the multi-sectoral marginal abatement cost. Journal of Cleaner Production. 2020;**253**:119945

[36] Gilmore EA, Ghosh M, Johnston P, et al. Modeling the energy mix and economic costs of deep decarbonization scenarios in a CGE framework. Energy and Climate Change. 2023;**4**:100106

[37] Babatunde KA, Begum RA, Said FF. Application of computable general equilibrium (CGE) to climate change mitigation policy: A systematic review. Renewable and Sustainable Energy Reviews. 2017;**78**:61-71

[38] Nicita L, Bosello F, Standardi G, et al. An integrated assessment of the impact of agrobiodiversity on the economy of the Euro-Mediterranean region. Ecological Economics. 2024;**218**:108125

[39] Ji CJ, Wang X, Wang XY, et al. Design and impact assessment of policies to overcome oversupply in China's national carbon market. Journal of Environmental Management. 2024;**354**:120388

[40] Wang T, Teng F, Zhang X. Assessing global and national economic losses from climate change: A study based on CGEM-IAM in China. Climate Change Economics. 2020;**11**(03):2041003

[41] Ciscar JC, Szabó L, Van Regemorter D, et al. The integration of PESETA sectoral economic impacts into the GEM-E3 Europe model: Methodology and results. Climatic Change. 2012;**112**:127-142

[42] Costantini V, Markandya A, Paglialunga E, et al. Impact and distribution of climatic damages: A methodological proposal with a dynamic CGE model applied to global climate negotiations. Economia Politica. 2018;**35**:809-843

[43] Eboli F, Parrado R, Roson R. Climate-change feedback on economic growth: Explorations with a dynamic general equilibrium model. Environment and Development Economics. 2010;**15**(5):515-533

[44] Dellink R, Lanzi E, Chateau J. The sectoral and regional economic consequences of climate change to 2060. Environmental and Resource Economics. 2019;**72**:309-363

[45] Babiker MHM, Reilly JM, Mayer M, et al. The MIT emissions prediction and policy analysis (EPPA) model: Revisions, sensitivities, and comparisons of results. Working Paper. 2001

[46] Fujimori S, Masui T, Matsuoka Y. AIM/CGE [Basic] Manual. Center for Social and Environmental Systems Research, NIES: Tsukuba, Japan; 2012

[47] Burniaux JM, Truong TP. GTAP-E: An energy-environmental version of the GTAP model. In: Global Trade Analysis Project (GTAP). West Lafayette: Purdue University; 2002

[48] Cong R, Han T, Wang P, et al. Advances and prospects in artificial intelligence for climate change governance. Journal of Beijing Institute of Technology (Social Sciences Edition). 2025;**27**(2):37-47

[49] Lamontagne JR, Reed PM, Link R, et al. Large ensemble analytic framework

for consequence-driven discovery of climate change scenarios. Earth's Future. 2018;**6**(3):488-504

[50] Kwakkel JH, Jaxa-Rozen M. Improving scenario discovery for handling heterogeneous uncertainties and multinomial classified outcomes. Environmental Modelling & Software. 2016;**79**:311-321

[51] Herman JD, Zeff HB, Lamontagne JR, et al. Synthetic drought scenario generation to support bottom-up water supply vulnerability assessments. Journal of Water Resources Planning and Management. 2016;**142**(11):04016050

[52] Camps-Valls G, Fernández-Torres MÁ, Cohrs KH, et al. Artificial intelligence for modeling and understanding extreme weather and climate events. Nature Communications. 2025;**16**(1):1919

[53] Vo TQ, Kim SH, Nguyen DH, et al. LSTM-CM: A hybrid approach for natural drought prediction based on deep learning and climate models. Stochastic Environmental Research and Risk Assessment. 2023;**37**(6):2035-2051

[54] Shi X. Enabling smart dynamical downscaling of extreme precipitation events with machine learning. Geophysical Research Letters. 2020;**47**(19):e2020GL090309

[55] Shi H, Li X, Wang S. How Bayesian networks are applied in the subfields of climate change: Hotspots and evolution trends. Environmental Modelling & Software. 2024;**172**:105921

[56] Crost B, Traeger CP. Optimal climate policy: Uncertainty versus Monte Carlo. Economics Letters. 2013;**120**(3):552-558

[57] Lee J, Cooley D, Wagner AM, et al. A calibration method for projecting future extremes via a linear mapping of parameters. Environmental and Ecological Statistics. 2025;**32**(1):1-20

[58] Elsaesser GS, van Lier-Walqui M, Yang Q, et al. Using machine learning to generate a GISS ModelE calibrated physics ensemble (CPE). Journal of Advances in Modeling Earth Systems. 2025;**17**(4):e2024MS004713

[59] Grimm V, Sölch C, Zöttl G. Emissions reduction in a second-best world: On the long-term effects of overlapping regulations. Energy Economics. 2022;**109**:105829

[60] Bhardwaj C, Axsen J, McCollum D. Which "second-best" climate policies are best? Simulating cost-effective policy mixes for passenger vehicles. Resource and Energy Economics. 2022;**70**:101319

[61] Wang C, Cai W, Zheng X, et al. Frontiers of climate policy research under carbon neutral goals. Journal of Beijing Institute of Technology (Social Sciences Edition). 2022;**24**(4):74-80

[62] Fawzy S, Osman AI, Doran J, et al. Strategies for mitigation of climate change: A review. Environmental Chemistry Letters. 2020;**18**:2069-2094

[63] Lemoine D. The climate risk premium: How uncertainty affects the social cost of carbon. Journal of the Association of Environmental and Resource Economists. 2021;**8**(1):27-57

[64] Tang BJ, Wang XY, Wei YM. Quantities versus prices for best social welfare in carbon reduction: A literature review. Applied Energy. 2019;**233**:554-564

Chapter 6

Distance Measure between Intuitionistic Fuzzy Sets with Its Application to TOPSIS and Decision-Making Problems

Vanita Rani and Satish Kumar

Abstract

Intuitionistic fuzzy sets (IFSs) are renowned for their exceptional ability to handle and express uncertain data due to their belonging to the fuzzy sets (FSs) generation. They have been widely implemented in various domains. However, the measurement of distance between (IFSs) remains a challenging and unresolved issue that has been the focus of research for many years. Despite numerous methods being proposed, they frequently yield unexpected results, lack discrimination, and fall short of the axiomatic definition of distance measures. We present a new IFS distance measure in this chapter. This novel measure has non-linear properties and satisfies the axiomatic definition of a distance measure. Consequently, it can accurately discern the disparities between IFSs and outperforms existing measures in generating rational results, as demonstrated by several numerical examples. The suggested algorithm for multi-attribute decision-making (MADM) leverages these benefits and provides a promising solution for addressing inference problems.

Keywords: intuitionistic fuzzy sets, distance measure, similarity measures, TOPSIS, multi-attribute decision making

1. Introduction

Due to the complexity of the choice environment, decision-makers frequently face some ambiguous information while solving MADM problems, which is utilized to characterize decision alternatives. Hence, the treatment of uncertain information will affect the decision results. To address ambiguous information effectively, Zadeh [1] suggested the theory of fuzzy sets. Numerous researchers have since verified the practical applicability of fuzzy sets in handling imprecise data. However, it cannot separately express the negative and rejected information. Aiming at this issue, various extensions of the *FSs* have been given. Atanassov [2] extended the *FSs* to the *IFSs*. Atanassov and Gargor [3] proved that *IFSs* and interval-valued fuzzy sets (*IVFSs*) are equipotent. Due to the ability of *IFSs* to deal with vagueness, It has found extensive application in diverse domains like decision-making, identifying patterns, and aiding in medical diagnoses [4–7]. Li [8, 9] research in the area of MADM brought forth pioneering investigations. These studies introduced fresh methodologies that expand upon established techniques by integrating non-linear programming using Technique for Order Preference by Similarity to an Ideal Solution (TOPSIS) and closeness coefficients. In a similar vein, Chen and Chiou [10] presented their own MADM methodologies. Their work aims to overcome limitations in existing decision-making approaches, such as the "division by zero problem," which can impede obtaining preference orders for alternatives in certain situations. Furthermore, Chen and Huang [11] introduced a new MADM technique that relies on IVIFSs and linear programming methodology. Their approach addresses some of the shortcomings observed in Chen and Chiou's [10] methodology. In a separate study, Zeng [12] introduced an innovative MADM technique in their study. This novel approach leverages non-linear programming alongside the TOPSIS method. The primary objective of their research was to address the limitations associated with the strategy proposed by Wang et al. [13].

Distance metrics play a crucial role in assessing the level of similarity and dissimilarity between pairs of objects. These valuable tools have found applications across diverse domains, including decision-making and cluster analysis Rakhi Gupta and Satish Kumar [14, 15]. In our everyday interactions, we frequently come across scenarios demanding a comparison between two entities, calling for a clear distinction between them. This requirement has given rise to diverse comparative techniques, and among them, the fuzzy set comparison framework stands out as a prevalent approach. The utilization of FSs and IFSs is widespread across numerous mathematical problem domains.

Zadeh [1] pioneering contributions to FSs have made significant strides across diverse fields. The bounded nature of each FS's element between 0 and 1 aligns well with real-world scenarios, emphasizing its relevance in addressing practical issues. The conceptual underpinning of FSs holds paramount importance in handling such challenges. This foundation was extended by Atanassov through the introduction of IFSs, which incorporated non-membership degrees Atanassov [2], maintaining values within the 0 to 1 range. Building upon this, researchers like Montes [16]; Rakhi and Satish [14, 15] advanced the scope of IFSs by proposing measures of similarity and dissimilarity. A plethora of studies by Arya and Kumar [17], Rakhi Gupta and Satish [14, 15] have delved into the utilization of both IFSs and FSs.

Vanita [18–20] and Arya and Kumar [21] delved into cross-entropy and similarity measures leveraging these measures in the context of Multiple Criteria Decision Making (MCDM). On the contrary, Dinh et al. [22] and his collaborators presented an alternative concept in their work, suggesting a dissimilarity measure. Another advancement, the correlation coefficient, was innovatively introduced by [4, 23]. This measure has exhibited its usefulness across diverse domains like clustering, pattern recognition, and medical contexts. Furthermore, the challenges inherent in the field of MCDM were tackled by researchers ([5–7]; Li, [8, 9]).

The chapter's key motivations are:

1. To introduce and verify a novel distance measure.

2. The proposed approaches' effectiveness and superiority can be demonstrated by illustrating how the suggested distance measure resolves counter-intuitive cases that are not addressed by established approaches.

3. An algorithm has been developed for solving MADM problems, which utilizes the proposed distance as a basis.

The rest of the chapter is as follows: In the "Preliminaries" section, we lay the groundwork by introducing key definitions, delving into the theory of *FSs* and *IFSs*, and exploring dissimilarity measures or distance metrics. In the "Proposed Measure" segment, we unveil an innovative distance metric. The efficacy of this new metric is assessed through a "Comparison Study," where it is juxtaposed against existing alternatives using numerical examples. Moving forward, we delve into the "TOPSIS Approach" and its practical application. Additionally, we explore the practical implementation of the "MADM Application" through mathematical demonstrations. The culmination of our work, along with insights into future directions, finds its place in the "Conclusion" section.

2. Preliminaries

In the preliminary, we provided essential definitions, notations, and a comprehensive analysis of the theories associated with *FS* and *IFS*.

Definition 1.1 Zadeh [1] *suggested FS* M^*. *In a discrete universal set* $U = \{u_1, u_2, \dots, u_n\}$

$$M^* = \{(u_m, z_M{}^*(u_m))\backslash u_m \in U\}, m = 1, 2, \dots, n. \tag{1}$$

where $r_M{}^*(u_m)$ indicates the membership of the ingredient $u_m \in U$, such that $0 \le r_M{}^*(u_m) \le 1$.

Definition 1.2 Atanassov [2] *suggested IFS* M^* *in a set U, as follows*

$$M^* = \{(u_m, r_M{}^*(u_m), l_M{}^*(u_m))\backslash u_m \in U\}, m = 1, 2, \dots, n. \tag{2}$$

where $r_M{}^*(u_m)$ is the membership and $l_M{}^*(u_m))$ is non-membership of the elements $u_m \in U$ in the set M^* such that $0 \le r_M{}^*(u_m) + l_M{}^*(u_m) \le 1$. Here, $h_M{}^*(u_m) = 1 - r_M{}^*(u_m) - l_M{}^*(u_m)$ denotes the hesitancy degree.

Definition 1.3 Coung and Pham [24], For every two *IFSs* M_1 and M_2, some operations are given below:

1. $M_1 \subseteq M_2$ iff $\forall\, u_m \in U$, $r_{M1}(u_m) \le r_{M2}(u_m)$, $l_{M1}(u_m) \le l_{M2}(u_m)$;

2. $M_1 = M_2$ iff $\forall\, u_m \in U$, $M_1 \subseteq M_2$ and $M_2 \subseteq M_1$;

3. $(M_1)^c = \{(u_m, l_{M1}(u_m), h_{M1}(u_m), r_{M1}(u_m) \,/\, u_m \in U)\}$.

Definition 1.4 Van Dinh [22] Distance measure V_P^*:$IFS(U)x\ IFS(U) \to [0,1]$ is a distance measure function on $IFS(U)$, on the condition that it holds properties:

1. $(P1) 0 \le V_P^*(M_1, M_2) \le 1$.

2. $(P2) V_P^*(M_1, M_1) = 0$

3. $(P3) V_P^*(M_1, M_2) = V_P^*(M_2, M_1)$.

4. $(P4)$if $M_1 \subseteq M_2 \subseteq M_3$ then $V_P^*(M_1, M_3) \ge \text{Max}\{V_P^*(M_1, M_3), V_P^*(M_2, M_3)\}$.

3. Existing distance measures

Atanassov [2], gave the distance measure (3)-(6), for *IFSs*, M_1 and M_2.
Hamming Distance

$$IA_H^*(M_1, M_2) = \frac{1}{2}\sum_{i=1}^{q}(|r_{M_1}(u_i) - r_{B_2}(u_i)| + |l_{M_1}(u_i) - l_{M_2}(u_i)|) \tag{3}$$

Normalized Distance

$$IA_{NH}^*(M_1, M_2) = \frac{1}{2q}\sum_{i=1}^{q}(|r_{M_1}(u_i) - r_{M_2}(u_i)| + |l_{M_1}(u_i) - l_{M_2}(u_i)|) \tag{4}$$

Euclidean Distance

$$IA_{ED}^*(M_1, M_2) = \left(\sum_{i=1}^{t}\frac{1}{2}\left[(r_{M_1}(u_i) - r_{M_2}(u_i))^2 + (l_{M_1}(u_i) - l_{M_2}(u_i))^2\right]\right)^{\frac{1}{2}} \tag{5}$$

Normalized Euclidean Distance

$$IA_{NED}^*(M_1, M_2) = \left(\sum_{i=1}^{t}\frac{1}{2t}\left[(r_{M_1}(u_i) - r_{M_2}(u_i))^2 + (l_{M_1}(u_i) - l_{M_2}(u_i))^2\right]\right)^{\frac{1}{2}} \tag{6}$$

Szmidt and Kacprzyk [25], gave the distance measures (7)-(10) by adding intuitionistic fuzzy index $r(k_i)$,
Hamming Distance

$$IS_H^*(M_1, M_2) = \frac{1}{2}\sum_{i=1}^{t}(|l_{M_1}(u_i) - l_{M_2}(u_i)| + |m_{M_1}(u_i) - m_{M_2}(u_i)| + |r_{M_1}(u_i) - r_{M_2}(u_i)|) \tag{7}$$

Normalized Hamming Distance

$$f_{NH}^*(M_1, M_2) = \frac{1}{2t}\sum_{i=1}^{t}(|l_{M_1}(u_i) - l_{M_2}(u_i)| + |m_{M_1}(u_i) - m_{M_2}(u_i)| + |r_{M_1}(u_i) - r_{M_2}(u_i)|) \tag{8}$$

Euclidean Distance

$$IS_{ED}^*(M_1, M_2) = \left(\frac{1}{2}\sum_{i=1}^{t}\left((l_{M_1}(u_i) - l_{M_2}(u_i))^2 + (m_{M_1}(u_i) - m_{M_2}(u_i))^2 + (r_{M_1}(u_i) - r_{M_2}(u_i))^2\right)\right)^{\frac{1}{2}} \tag{9}$$

Normalized Euclidean Distance

$$IS_{NED}^*(M_1, M_2) = \left(\frac{1}{2t}\sum_{i=1}^{t}\left((l_{M_1}(u_i) - l_{M_2}(u_i))^2 + (m_{M_1}(u_i) - m_{M_1}(u_i))^2 + (r_{M_1}(u_i) - r_{M_2}(u_i))^2\right)\right)^{\frac{1}{2}} \tag{10}$$

Wang and Xin [26] **Distance measure**

$$IW^*_{FW1}(M_1,M_2) = \frac{1}{t}\sum_{i=1}^{t} \left[\frac{(|l_{M_1}(u_i) - l_{M_2}(u_i)| + |m_{M_1}(u_i) - m_{M_2}(u_i)|)}{4} + \frac{max\,(|l_{M_1}(u_i) - l_{M_2}(u_i)|, |m_{M_1}(u_i) - m_{M_2}(u_i)|)}{2}\right] \quad (11)$$

$$IW^*_{FW2}(M_1,M_2) = \frac{1}{t}\sum_{i=1}^{t}\left(\frac{|l_{M_1}(u_i) - l_{M_2}(u_i)| + |m_{M_1}(u_i) - m_{M_2}(u_i)|}{2}\right) \quad (12)$$

Grzegorzewski's [27] **Distance measure**

$$I^*_{GD}(M_1,M_2) = \frac{1}{t}\left(\sum_{i=1}^{q} max\,(|l_{M_1}(u_i) - l_{M_2}(u_i)|, |m_{M_1}(u_i) - m_{M_2}(u_i)|)\right) \quad (13)$$

Yang and Chiclana [28] **Distance measure**

$$I^*_{YF}(M_1,M_2) = \frac{1}{t}\left(\sum_{i=1}^{t} max\,(|l_{M_1}(u_i) - l_{M_2}(u_i)|, |m_{M_1}(u_i) - m_{M_2}(u_i)|, |r_{M_1}(u_i) - r_{M_2}(u_i)|)\right) \quad (14)$$

Grzegorzewski's [27] **Distance measure**
Hamming Distance

$$IG^*_{H}(M_1,M_2) = \sum_{i=1}^{t} \max\left\{\left|l^2_{M_1}(u_i) - l^2_{M_2}(u_i)\right|, \left|m^2_{M_1}(u_i) - m^2_{M_2}(u_i)\right|\right\} \quad (15)$$

Normalized Hamming Distance

$$IG^*_{NH}(M_1,M_2) = \frac{1}{t}\sum_{i=1}^{t} \max\left\{\left|l^2_{M_1}(u_i) - l^2_{M_2}(u_i)\right|, \left|m^2_{M_1}(u_i) - m^2_{M_2}(u_i)\right|\right\} \quad (16)$$

Euclidean Distance

$$IG^*_{ED}(M_1,M_2) = \left(\sum_{i=1}^{q} \max\left[\left(l^2_{M_1}(u_i) - l^2_{M_2}(k_i)\right)^2, \left(m^2_{M_1}(u_i) - m^2_{M_2}(u_i)\right)^2\right]\right)^{\frac{1}{2}} \quad (17)$$

Normalized Euclidean Distance

$$IG^*_{NED}(M_1,M_2) = \left(\frac{1}{t}\sum\nolimits_{i=1}^{t} \max\left[\left(l^2_{M_1}(u_i) - l^2_{M_2}(u_i)\right)^2, \left(m^2_{M_1}(u_i) - m^2_{M_2}(u_i)\right)^2\right]\right)^{\frac{1}{2}} \quad (18)$$

4. Proposed distance measure (for IF-environment)

Numerous researchers have proposed a range of distance metrics for IFSs. However, some of these metrics exhibit shortcomings in their ability to facilitate well-founded decision-making. In light of these limitations, we can classify these metrics into two categories: those that produce identical results and those that result in contradictory and illogical outcomes. There exists a need for a more effective formulation of distance metrics to overcome these drawbacks. Thus, we aimed to develop an innovative and dependable distance metric that could more effectively manage diverse practical scenarios and offer enhanced credibility.

Let U be universal set for two IFSs M_1 and M_2. Now, we interpret a distance measure $V_P^*: IFS(U) \times IFS(U) \to [0,1]$ as below:

$$V_P^*(M_1, M_2) = \frac{1}{t}\sum_{m=1}^{t}\left[\frac{1}{1 + min\,(1, |r_{M_1}(u_m) - r_{M_2}(u_m)|, |l_{M_1}(u_m) - l_{M_2}(u_m)|)}\right] \quad (19)$$

Theorem 1.1 Proposed measure $V_P^*(M_1, M_2)$ satisfy the properties of definition 1.4.

1. $(P1)$For $M_1, M_2 \in IFS(W)$, it is evident $0 \leq |rm_1(u_m) - r_{M2}(u_m)|, |l_{M1}(u_m) - l_{M2}(u_m)|) \leq 1$ $0 \leq \min\{|r_{M1}(u_m) - r_{m2}(u_m)|, |l_{M7}(u_m) - l_{M2}(u_m)|)\} \leq 1$

   Suppose $x_i = \min(1,|r_{M1}(u_m) - r_{M2}(u_m)|)$ or $\min(1,|l_{M1}(u_m) - l_{M2}(u_m)|)$ since $0 \leqslant x_i \leqslant 1$, then $0 \leq \frac{1}{1+x_i} \leq 1, \forall x_i \in [0,1]$.

   Hence $0 \leq V_p^*(M_1, M_2) \leq 1$.

2. $(P2)$If $M_1 = M_2$ then $r_{M1}(u_m) = r_{M2}(u_m), l_{M1}(u_m) = l_{M2}(u_m)$ for all u_m. therefore, $|r_{M1}(u_m) - r_{M2}(u_m)| = |\,l_{M1}(u_m) - l_{M2}(u_m)| = |_{M1}(u_m) - _{M2}(u_m)| = 0$, This gives $V_p^*(M_1, M_2) = 0$.

3. $(P3)$It is obvious.

4. $(P4)$If $M_1 \subseteq M_2 \subseteq M_3$, then $r_{M1}(u_m) \leq r_{M2}(u_m) \leq r_{M3}(u_m)$ $l_{M1}(u_m) \geq l_{M2}(u_m) \geq l_{M3}(u_m)$ for all $w_i \in U$.

$$|\,r_{M1}(u_m) - r_{M2}(u_m)| \leq |r_{M1}(u_m) - r_{M3}(u_m)|, ||r_{M2}(u_m) - r_{M3}(u_m)| \leq |r_{M1}(u_m) - r_{M3}(u_m)|$$

$$|l_{M1}(u_m) - l_{M2}(u_m)| \leq |l_{M1}(u_m) - l_{M3}(u_m)|, |l_{M2}(u_m) - l_{M3}(u_m)| \leq |l_{M1}(u_m) - l_{M3}(u_m)|$$

This implies $\min\{|r_{M1}(u_m) - r_{M2}(u_m)|, |l_{M1}(u_m) - l_{M2}(u_m)|\} \leq \min\{|r_{M1}(u_m) - r_{M3}(u_m)|, |l_{M1}(u_m) - l_{M3}(u_m)|\}$

$$\forall x_i, y_i \in [0, 1], x_i \leq y_i,$$

Now $\frac{1}{1+x_i} \leq \frac{1}{1+y_i}$. This proves the inequality $V_p^*(M_1, M_3) \geq V_p^*(M_1, M_2)$.

Similarly, we can prove $V_p^*(M_1, M_3) \geq V_p^*(M_1, M_2)$

Now, we assign a weight $w_i \in [0,1]$, $\sum_{i=1}^{t} w_i = 1$. We introduce an innovative distance metric for comparing two *IFSs* as follows.

Definition 1.2 We define a distance measure $V_{NP}^*: IFS(U) \times XIFS(U) \to [0,1]$ as below:

$$V_{NP}{}^*(M_1, M_2) = \sum_{i=1}^{t} w_i V_P^*(M_1, M_2) \quad (20)$$

Theorem 1.3 Proposed measure $V_{NP}^*(M_1, M_2)$ satisfy the properties of definition 1.4.

Proof: Proof is clear from Theorem 1.1.

5. Comparative study

Example 1.1 Consider the problem where the picture fuzzy sets are $O = (0.4, 0.6)$, $B = (0.5, 0.5)$, $C = (0.6, 0.3)$ and $D = (0.7, 0.3)$. The problem is to solve the distance metrics between A and B, C, D and find which of B, C and D is more closer to A. The pair (A, B), (A, C), (A, D) whose distance is very low considered as considered as perfect dissimilarity, if any distances are equal then the pairs (A, B), (A, C), (A, D) is indistinguishable. From the **Table 1** these distances IA^*_H, IA^*_{NH}, IA^*_{Ed}, IA^*_{NED}, IS^*_H, IS^*_{NH}, IS^*_{Ed}, IS^*_{NED}, IW^*_{FW1}, IW^*_{FW2}, I^*_{GD}, I^*_{YF}, IG^*_H, IG^*_{NH}, IG^*_{Ed}, IG^*_{NED}, are not effective because any two distances are equal. Suggested distance measure V_P^* is distinguishable because ***IFS B*** is lower distance to A in comparison with C and D. Therefore, it can be said that the suggested measures V_P^* is more sensible and better than existing distance measures IA^*_H, IA^*_{NH}, IA^*_{Ed}, IA^*_{NED}, IS^*_H, IS^*_{NH}, IS^*_{Ed}, IS^*_{NED}, IW^*_{FW1}, IW^*_{FW2}, I^*_{GD}, I^*_{YF}, IG^*_H, IG^*_{NH}, IG^*_{Ed}, IG^*_{NED}

6. TOPSIS approach

We shall employ the approach known as the Technique for Order Preference by Similarity to an Ideal Solution (TOPSIS), as introduced in [29]. This methodology proves valuable when dealing with issues related to incomplete data concerning criteria weights. Let $P = \{P_1, P_2, \dots P_m\}$ be the set of **m** alternatives. To address the decision-making process for choosing the most suitable ranking the alternatives in

Cases	(A, B)	(A, C)	(A, D)	*Comment*
V^*_P	0.1818	0.3333	0.4615	Distinguishable, B
IA^*_H	0.1000	0.3000	0.3000	Not effective
IA^*_{NH}	0.1000	0.3000	0.3000	Not effective
IA^*_{Ed}	0.1100	0.3300	0.3300	Not effective
IA^*_{NED}	0.1100	0.3300	0.3300	Not effective
IS^*_H	0.1200	0.2500	0.2500	Not effective
IS^*_{NH}	0.1200	0.2500	0.2500	Not effective
IS^*_{ED}	0.1732	0.1732	0.0400	Not effective
IS^*_{NED}	0.1100	0.3300	0.3300	Not effective
IW^*_{FW1}	0.1000	0.2750	0.2750	Not effective
IW^*_{FW2}	0.1100	0.2500	0.2500	Not effective
I^*_{GD}	0.1000	0.3000	0.3000	Not effective
I^*_{YF}	0.1000	0.3000	0.3000	Not effective
IG^*_H	0.1100	0.3300	0.3300	Not effective
IG^*_{NH}	0.1100	0.3300	0.3300	Not effective
IG^*_{ED}	0.1000	0.3000	0.3000	Not effective
IG^*_{NED}	0.1000	0.3000	0.3000	Not effective

Table 1.
Enumeration of various distance measures.

order of preference from the given set P, considering the criteria set $T = \{T_1, T_2, \ldots. T_n\}$, we introduce the IF-decision matrix $B = [b_{ij}]_{m \times n}$. In this context, the variables i and j correspond to IF-numbers assigned by decision-makers, denoting the diverse assessment scores for each alternative P_i concerning every criterion T_j. In this context, we propose an extension of the TOPSIS method tailored to address MADM problems. This extension involves utilizing our newly devised intuitionistic fuzzy weighted distance, denoted by Eq. (20), while taking into account the incomplete information pertaining to the weights of the criteria. The ensuing steps outline our approach for handling these situations:

Step 1: We begin by constructing the IF-decision matrix denoted as $B = [b_{ij}]_{m \times n}$. In this matrix, each entry b_{ij} represents the various evaluation values provided by the decision-makers, indicating the extent to which the alternative P_i fulfills the criteria T_j.

Step 2: In cases where the information concerning criteria weights is incomplete, we present a novel approach to ascertain these weights. Our method involves determining the criteria weights using the following formula:

$$w_j = \frac{\frac{\max(b_j) + \min(b_j)}{2}}{\sum_{j=1}^{n} \frac{\max(b_j) + \min(b_j)}{2}}$$

Step 3: In the conventional TOPSIS method, the evaluation criteria are typically categorized into two groups: benefit criteria and cost criteria. Let us denote the set of benefit criteria as R_1 and the set of cost criteria as R_2. Embracing the principles of IF-theory within the concept of TOPSIS, we introduce the concept of the positive ideal solution (PIS) denoted as F^+ and the negative ideal solution (NIS) denoted as F^-, which are defined as follows: $F^+ = \{(T_j, b_j^+): T_j \in T\}$ and $F^- = \{(T_j, b_j^-): T_j \in T\}$, where $b_j^+ = \{1\}$, $b_j^- = \{0\}$, $j \in R_1$ and $b_j^+ = \{0\}$, $b_j^- = \{1\}$, $j \in R_2$.

Step 4: To quantify the distances between each alternative P_i and the F_+, as well as the F^-, we introduce the concept of IFS based on our proposed intuitionistic fuzzy weighted Hausdorff distance defined in Eq. (20). The IFS for each alternative is calculated as follows:

$$D^+(B_i) = V^*{}_{NP}(B_i, F^+) \text{and } D^-(B_i) = V^*{}_{NP}(B_i, F^-), i = 1, 2, \ldots m.$$

Step 5: To evaluate the proximity and rank the alternatives, the relative closeness coefficient comes into play. This coefficient measures the relative closeness of each alternative to the PIS and the NIS. A higher relative closeness coefficient signifies that an alternative is closer to the PIS while being farther from the NIS. The computation of the relative closeness degree $D^+(B_i)$ for each alternative P_i in relation to the intuitionistic fuzzy ideal solutions is accomplished using the following formula:

$$D(B_i) = \frac{D^-}{D^- + D^+}$$

Ultimately, the alternatives are ranked in order of preference based on their degrees of closeness. The alternative that attains the highest value of the degree of closeness will be regarded as the most preferred alternative among the set of choices.

Example 1.3 In the current era, when the mean income of the household is rising there is increased demand of consumption of electricity/energy both for the common houses and for the industry. However, the generation of power is associated with negative environmental effects win terms of pollution which has been objected by various awareness groups and also the government is committed to bring down the carbon footprints for improving their international image. The Government thus has decided to increase the production through use of renewable power generation plants which could be solar, wind, hydro or geothermal.

Government has proposed to issue a request for proposal from the highly competent energy production companies dealing in renewable energy generation for which they have identified five most capable companies as partners. The assessment of their performance is planned to be carried out using five different criteria. The five key partners chosen by the government are listed above: The alternatives are as follows:

a. Tata Power – P1

b. Adani Energy – P2

c. Reliance Power – P3

d. Vedanta energy solutions – P4

e. Kirloskar – P5

The five most important criteria to select the power companies are elaborated below **Table 2**.

Imagine a group of decision-makers made up of five specialized individuals. Their objective is to evaluate different options and choose the best one according to certain criteria. The assessments of these options, labeled as P_i, in relation to the criteria T_j have been documented in a table referred to as **Table 3**. This collection of evaluations is organized into a matrix named *B*, which represents an intuitionistic fuzzy decision matrix, and its elements are denoted as $B = [b_{ij}]_{5 \times 5}$. As the information about the criteria weights w_j remains unknown, Step 2 is utilized to compute the weights w_j for each criterion T_j. This involves employing the proposed method based on intuitionistic fuzzy weighted distance as described in Eq. (20). By employing this technique, we derive the Intuitionistic Separation Measures F^+ and F^-, presented in matrices. These Integrated Sustainability Measures play a pivotal role in establishing the comparative

Criteria	Description
Cost per unit (T1)	Cost borne by the end user per unit.
Environment rating (T2)	The rating given by the accredited agency to the company for its operation and environmental effects.
Capital of the company (T3)	The size of the company, its balance sheet, profitability, and asset holdings.
Experience (T4)	Number of years of experience and service satisfaction.
Technical competence (T5)	The technical capability of the company in efficiently producing the power and transmission to the load center

Table 2.
Description of Criteria.

	T_1	T_2	T_3	T_4	T_5
P_1	(0.3,0.5)	(0.4,0.5)	(0.5,0.2)	(0.4,0.3)	(0.1,0.5)
P_2	(0.2,0.7)	(0.4,0.4)	(0.5,0.3)	(0.7,0.1)	(0.2,0.7)
P_3	(0.5,0.5)	(0.8,0.1)	(0.3,0.2)	(0.1,0.6)	(0.6,0.0)
P_4	(0.0,1.0)	(0.9,0.1)	(0.2,0.5)	(0.6,0.3)	(0.0,0.7)
P_5	(0.8,0.1)	(0.5,0.3)	(0.5,0.4)	(0.2,0.8)	(0.5,0.4)

Table 3.
Intuitionistic fuzzy decision matrix.

	$D^+(B_i)$	$D^-(B_i)$	$D(B_i)$	*Ranking*
P_1	0.1768	0.1926	0.5214	4
P_2	0.2197	0.2042	0.4817	1
P_3	0.1421	0.1560	0.5233	5
P_4	0.1694	0.1602	0.4860	2
P_5	0.1238	0.1333	0.5185	3

Table 4.
ISM and relative closeness degree.

levels of proximity that each option holds concerning the intuitionistic fuzzy ideal solutions.

Once the relative proximity values are established for all potential alternatives, we proceed to arrange them in a ranked order of preference. The choice that attains the highest relative proximity coefficient is designated as the optimal selection. In the context outlined in **Table 4**, the alternative denoted as P_3 emerges as the prime choice. This decision stems from its remarkable closeness to the F^+ while simultaneously maintaining a considerable distance from the F^-.

It's important to highlight that the second step of this process is utilized to calculate the weights assigned to the criteria (w_j) when no prior information is available about them. This computation leads to the following weight values: $w_1 = 0.225$, $w_2 = 0.250$, $w_3 = 0.175$, $w_4 = 0.200$, and $w_5 = 0.150$.

On the whole, this practical illustration underscores the efficacy of the suggested distance measurement technique for MCDM, particularly when confronted with incomplete data pertaining to criterion weights. This methodology serves as a valuable instrument for decision-makers, aiding them in pinpointing the optimal alternative, even within situations characterized by information gaps **Figure 1**.

Then PIS F^+ and NIS F^- are given as

$$F^+ = \begin{bmatrix} \max(0.3, 0.2, 0.5, 0.0, 0.8), & \min(0.5, 0.7, 0.5, 1.0, 0.1) \\ \max(0.4, 0.4, 0.8, 0.9, 0.5), & \min(0.5, 0.4, 0.1, 0.1, 0.3) \\ \max(0.5, 0.5, 0.3, 0.2, 0.5), & \min(0.2, 0.3, 0.2, 0.5, 0.4) \\ \max(0.4, 0.7, 0.1, 0.6, 0.2), & \min(0.3, 0.1, 0.6, 0.3, 0.8) \\ \max(0.1, 0.2, 0.6, 0.0, 0.5), & \min(0.5, 0.7, 0.0, 0.7, 0.4) \end{bmatrix}$$

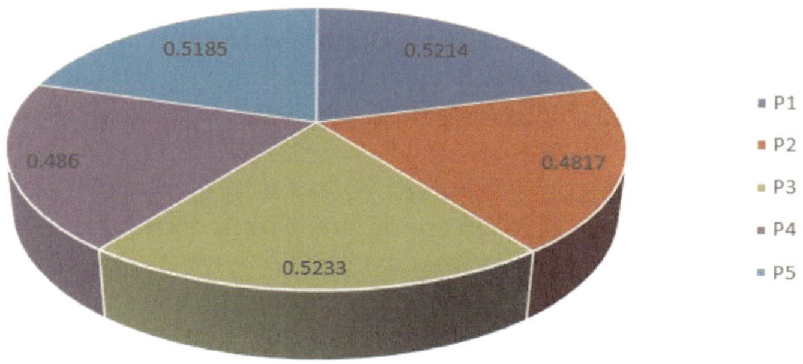

Figure 1.
Graph of ranking of alternatives.

$$F^{+} = \{(0.8, 0.1), (0.9, 0.1), (0.5, 0.2), (0.7, 0.1), (0.6, 0.0)\}$$

$$F^{-} = \begin{bmatrix} \min(0.3, 0.2, 0.5, 0.0, 0.8), & \max(0.5, 0.7, 0.5, 1.0, 0.1) \\ \min(0.4, 0.4, 0.8, 0.9, 0.5), & \max(0.5, 0.4, 0.1, 0.1, 0.3) \\ \min(0.5, 0.5, 0.3, 0.2, 0.5), & \max(0.2, 0.3, 0.2, 0.5, 0.4) \\ \min(0.4, 0.7, 0.1, 0.6, 0.2), & \max(0.3, 0.1, 0.6, 0.3, 0.8) \\ \min(0.1, 0.2, 0.6, 0.0, 0.5), & \max(0.5, 0.7, 0.0, 0.7, 0.4) \end{bmatrix}$$

$$F^{-} = \{(0.0, 0.7), (0.4, 0.5), (0.2, 0.5), (0.1, 0.8), (0.0, 0.7)\}$$

6.1 Comparative analysis

To ensure the legitimacy and efficiency of the TOPSIS methodology, we direct attention to **Table 5**. The table clearly demonstrates that, among all the existing methods, P_3 stands out as the optimal choice. This outcome is consistent with the results obtained from our proposed method, confirming its alignment with established approaches.

6.2 The weakness of TOPSIS approach

A widely recognized and successful method for tackling MADM problems is the TOPSIS, initially proposed by Hwang and Yoon [29], and later, it was expanded into

Different methods	Ranking	Best alternative
IFS-CODAS [30]	$P_2 > P_4 > P_5 > P_1 > P_3$	P_3
IFS-TOPSIS [31]	$P_2 > P_4 > P_5 > P_1 > P_3$	P_3
TODIM method [32]	$P_2 > P_4 > P_1 > P_5 > P_3$	P_3
EDAS method [33]	$P_2 > P_1 > P_5 > P_4 > P_3$	P_3
VIKOR method [34]	$P_2 > P_4 > P_5 > P_1 > P_3$	P_3
Proposed Method	$P_2 > P_4 > P_5 > P_1 > P_3$	P_3

Table 5.
Comparison study.

the fuzzy domain by Chen [35]. TOPSIS operates on the premise that the preferred alternative should be as close as possible to the PIS while simultaneously being as far as possible from the NIS. Despite its popularity, TOPSIS can sometimes fall short in achieving the ideal distance from the NIS, as demonstrated in the example above.

To address this limitation and offer a novel and improved approach to MADM, we propose a new and innovative MADM technique. This technique aims to refine the evaluation process, ensuring that the selected alternative genuinely maintains the desired distance from the NIS, thereby enhancing the quality of decision-making in complex scenarios.

7. MADM approach

To affirm the suitability of the distance metric for *IFSs*, practical experiments are commonly conducted. This section is dedicated to demonstrating the reliability of the suggested distance measure through the utilization of MADM problems. The findings affirm that the suggested distance measure aligns with logical reasoning and conforms to human thought processes.

Algorithm.

Let $U = \{u_1, u_2, \dots u_q\}$ be a set of attributes.

$P_i = P_{iq} = \{(u_q, r_{Pi}(u_q), l_{pi}(u_q)) | u_q \in U\}, i = 1,2, \dots ,n; q = 1,2, \dots ,t$. A multi-step decision-making procedure is used to identify the best alternative.

Step 1. Normalize decision alternatives.

In MADM cases, criteria are frequently divided into two groups: benefit type and cost type. The following formula should be used during the decision-making process to convert the cost attribute into a benefit attribute. There is no need for conversion if every criterion is already favorable:

$$\overline{P_{im}} = \begin{cases} P_{iq}, & \text{forbenefitattribute} u_q, \\ P^c_{iq}, & \text{forcostattribute} u_q, \end{cases} \tag{21}$$

$$P^c_{iq} = \{(u_q, r_{P_i}(u_q), l_{P_i}(u_q)) | u_q \in U\}, q = 1, 2, \dots, t.$$

The alternative R_i can be rewritten as $P_i = \overline{P_{iq}}$, which is based on the transformation formula above.

Step2. Calculate the distance measure $V^*_{NP}(P_i,P)$, $(i = 1, 2, \dots ..n)$, where $P = \overbrace{(1,0),(1,0),\dots,(1,0)}^{q}$ is an optimal alternative with q criteria.

Step 3. Choose the minimum one $D^*(P_{i0}, P)$ from $D^*(P_i, P)$ $(i = 1,2,3 \dots .,n)$, that is, $D^*(P_{i0}, P) = \min D^*(P_i, P)$.

The alternative P_{i0} is determined to be the optimal choice based on the principle of minimum distance measure.

Step 4. Calculate the degree of (DOC), $DOC = \sum_{i=1}^{n} |D^*(P_{i0}, P) - D(P_i, P)|$ [36]. The efficiency of a measure is based on the size of its DOC values, so this parameter is more important when evaluating the performance of various measures. If the DOC is the highest distance, the distance measure's conclusion is more reliable.

7.1 Applications for multi-attribute decision-making

Example 1.4 Due to increased supply and new incoming brands of Air conditioners the home users face increased difficulty in selecting the best air conditioner for their personal use. All these air conditioners comes with their unique selling points ranging from low power consumption, environmental friendly gases, cooling at high ambient temperatures, humidity controller etc. These highly technical points confuse the home users to opt for the best product. The Society of heating and refrigeration engineers has decided to club most important parameters to predict and select the best performing air conditioners for a general user, that would give the user satisfaction in colling and also environmental friendly. They have come up with five possible Brand categories of AC satisfying the performance parameters, defined as: (a) LG- R_1, (b) Samsung - R_2, (c) Haire- R_3, (d) Voltas - R_4, (e) Bluestar - R_5. The proposed weighted distance formula, Eq. (19), is utilized to determine the distance from each alternative by utilizing the weights w_j (0.25, 0.0.5, 0.70). **Table 3** shows the result of five air conditioners. **Table 4** shows the outcomes of different distance measures. The Society of Engineers has taken three most important parameters to select the brands above, which are elaborated below **Tables 6** and 7:

From R_1, R_2, R_3, R_4, and R_5, we want to select the best option. The outcome of the computation and the decision are presented in **Table 8** and **Figure 2**. Although there are five very similar decision alternatives in this case, established on the principle of minimum distance measure, the alternative R_3 can be regarded as the best option with the help of the distance measures. Moreover, in order to illustrate the reliability of decision results, we consider the confident measure of some distance measures and give the outcomes in **Table 8** and **Figure 2**. We can easily see that the confident measure of the suggested distance measure V^*_P is highest than that of other distance metrics such as IA^*_H, IA^*_{NH}, IA^*_{Ed}, IA^*_{NED}, IS^*_H, IS^*_{NH}, IS^*_{Ed}, IS^*_{NED}, IW^*_{FW1}, IW^*_{FW2}, I^*_{GD}, I^*_{YF}, IG^*_H, IG^*_{NH}, IG^*_{Ed}, IG^*_{NED}. As a result, the suggested metric is practical and appropriate for making decisions.

Criteria	Description of criteria
Low power consumption	Power consumption per square meter of cooling
Environmental friendly	Use of non-polluting CFC Gases for cooling
Cost per ton	Lowest capital and running cost

Table 6.
Criteria to evaluate air conditioner.

	T_1	T_2	T_3
R_1	(t_1, 0.2, 0.5)	(t_2, 0.3, 0.7)	(t_3, 0.5,0.3)
R_2	(t_1, 0.4, 0.5)	(t_2, 0.3, 0.6)	(t_3, 0.5,0.5)
R_3	(t_1, 0.4, 0.4)	(t_2, 0.5, 0.4)	(t_3, 0.6,0.3)
R_4	(t_1, 0.7, 0.2)	(t_2, 0.1, 0.8)	(t_3, 0.0,0.7)
R_5	(t_1, 0.3, 0.4)	(t_2, 0.5, 0.3)	(t_3, 0.5,0.4)

Table 7.
Three alternatives with five different attributes.

D	D (R_1R)	D (R_2R)	D (R_3R)	D (R_4R)	D (R_5R)	Ranking	Best Alternative	Doc
V^*_P	0.7773	0.7418	0.6490	0.8629	0.9531	$R_3 < R_2 < R_1 < R_4 < R_5$	R_3	0.7391
IA^*_H	0.3381	0.4006	0.2875	0.6319	0.3594	$R_3 < R_1 < R_5 < R_2 < R_4$	R_3	0.5800
IA^*_{NH}	0.0968	0.1197	0.0841	0.2013	0.1074	$R_3 < R_1 < R_5 < R_2 < R_4$	R_3	0.1888
IA^*_{Ed}	0.8470	0.8487	0.7762	0.9624	0.8278	$R_3 < R_1 < R_5 < R_2 < R_4$	R_3	0.3811
IA^*_{NED}	0.6984	0.6829	0.6460	0.6830	0.6760	$R_3 < R_5 < R_2 < R_4 < R_1$	R_3	0.6279
IS^*_H	0.5850	0.5350	0.4550	0.8200	0.5500	$R_3 < R_5 < R_2 < R_4 < R_1$	R_3	0.6700
IS^*_{NH}	0.5850	0.5350	0.4550	0.8200	0.5500	$R_3 < R_5 < R_2 < R_4 < R_1$	R_3	0.6700
IS^*_{ED}	0.5969	0.6127	0.5291	0.8445	0.5899	$R_3 < R_5 < R_1 < R_2 < R_4$	R_3	0.3492
IS^*_{NED}	0.2800	0.2984	0.2423	0.4589	0.2811	$R_3 < R_5 < R_2 < R_4 < R_1$	R_3	0.3492
IW^*_{FW1}	0.1771	0.1758	0.1412	0.2533	0.1704	$R_3 < R_5 < R_1 < R_2 < R_4$	R_3	0.2118
IW^*_{FW2}	0.1099	0.1254	0.0888	0.2054	0.1123	$R_3 < R_1 < R_5 < R_2 < R_4$	R_3	0.4073
I^*_{GD}	0.1950	0.1783	0.1517	0.2733	0.1833	$R_3 < R_2 < R_5 < R_4 < R_1$	R_3	0.2231
I^*_{YF}	0.1950	0.1783	0.1517	0.2733	0.1833	$R_3 < R_5 < R_4 < R_1 < R_3$	R_3	0.2231
IG^*_H	0.8105	0.7805	0.6955	0.8770	0.7900	$R_3 < R_2 < R_5 < R_1 < R_4$	R_3	0.2210
IG^*_{NH}	0.2702	0.2602	0.2318	0.2923	0.2633	$R_3 < R_2 < R_5 < R_4 < R_1$	R_3	0.1588
IG^*_{ED}	0.3521	0.3453	0.3259	0.3729	0.3478	$R_3 < R_2 < R_5 < R_4 < R_1$	R_3	0.1145
IG^*_{NED}	0.1632	0.1612	0.1474	0.1881	0.1616	$R_3 < R_2 < R_5 < R_4 < R_1$	R_3	0.0845

Table 8.
Results of distance measures.

8. Conclusion

This chapter presents a novel approach to address decision-making problems by proposing a novel distance metric for IFSs. The central aim is to establish a method for gauging the separation between IFSs, harnessing the power of TOPSIS and MADM. The proposed method exhibits several desirable features, such as adhering to the axiomatic definition of a distance measure, having non-linear characteristics, better

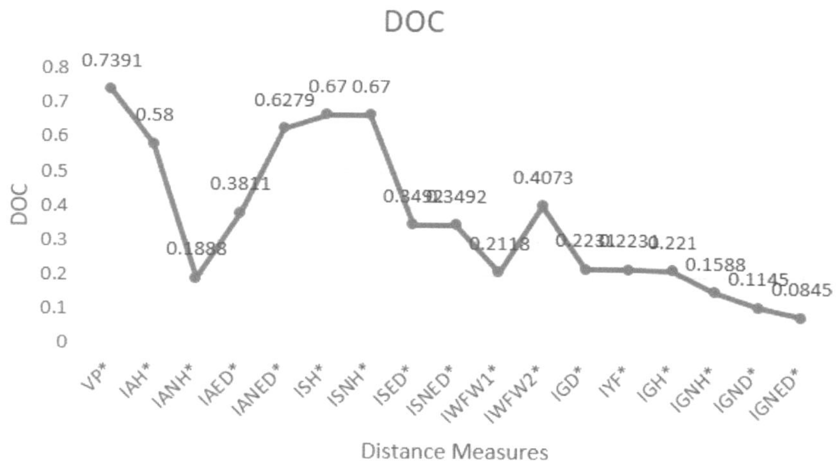

Figure 2.
Graph of DOC.

indicating the level of discrimination between IFSs, and avoiding counter-intuitive results. A MADM algorithm, designed based on these principles, effectively showcases the superiority of the suggested method when compared to existing distance metrics. The expansive applicability of this approach within the decision-making domain is evident. Future endeavors will extend this novel distance measure to more intricate scenarios involving interval-based IFSs.

Author details

Vanita Rani* and Satish Kumar
Maharishi Markandeshwar (Deemed To Be University), Mullana-Ambala, India

*Address all correspondence to: vanitanassa5279@gmail.com

References

[1] Zadeh LA. Fuzzy sets. Information Control. 1965;**8**(3):338-353

[2] Atanassov K. Intuitionistic fuzzy sets. Fuzzy Sets and Systems. 1986;**20**(1):87-96

[3] Atanassov K, Gargor G. Interval valued intuitionistic fuzzy sets. Fuzzy Sets and Systems. 1989;**31**(3):343-349

[4] Sanchez E. Medical diagnosis and composite advances. In: Fuzzy Set Theory and Applications. North Holland; 1979. pp. 437-444

[5] Jin J, Garg H. Intuitionistic fuzzy three-way ranking-based TOPSIS approach with a novel entropy measure and its application to medical treatment selection. Advances in Engineering Software. 2023;**180**:103459

[6] Li X, Liu Z, Han X, Liu N, Yuan W. An intuitionistic fuzzy version of Hellinger distance measure and its application to decision-making process. Symmetry. 2023;**15**(2):500

[7] Singh A, Kumar S. Novel fuzzy knowledge and accuracy measures with its applications in multi-criteria decision-making. Granular Computing. 2023;**8**(6):1-26

[8] Li DF. TOPSIS-based nonlinear-programming methodology for multiattribute decision making with interval-valued intuitionistic fuzzy sets. IEEE Transactions on Fuzzy Systems. 2010;**18**(2):299-311

[9] Li DF. Closeness coefficient based nonlinear programming method for interval-valued intuitionistic fuzzy multiattribute decision making with incomplete preference information. Applied Soft Computing. 2011;**11**(4): 3402-3418

[10] Chen SM, Chiou CH. Multiattribute decision making based on interval-valued intuitionistic fuzzy sets, PSO techniques, and evidential reasoning methodology. IEEE Transactions on Fuzzy Systems. 2014;**23**(6):1905-1916

[11] Chen SM, Huang ZC. Multiattribute decision making based on interval-valued intuitionistic fuzzy values and linear programming methodology. Information Sciences. 2017;**381**:341-351

[12] Zeng S, Chen SM, Fan KY. Interval-valued intuitionistic fuzzy multiple attribute decision making based on nonlinear programming methodology and TOPSIS method. Information Sciences. 2020;**506**:424-442

[13] Wang C, Zhou X, Tu H, Tao S. Some geometric aggregation operators based on picture fuzzy sets and their application in multiple attribute decision making. Italian Journal of Pure and Applied Mathematics. 2017;**37**:477-492

[14] Gupta R, Kumar S. Intuitionistic fuzzy similarity-based information measure in the application of pattern recognition and clustering. International Journal of Fuzzy Systems. 2022;**24**(5): 2493-2510

[15] Gupta R, Kumar S. Intuitionistic fuzzy scale-invariant entropy with correlation coefficients-based VIKOR approach for multi-criteria decision-making. Granular Computing. 2022;**7**(1): 77-93

[16] Montes S, Couso I, Gil P, Bertoluzza C. Divergence measure between fuzzy sets. International Journal of Approximate Reasoning. 2002;**30**(2):91-105

[17] Arya V, Kumar S. Fuzzy entropy measure with an applications in decision

making under bipolar fuzzy environment based on TOPSIS method. International Journal of Information and Management Sciences. 2020;**31**(2): 99-121

[18] Rani V, Kumar S. MCDM method for evaluating and ranking the online shopping websites based on a novel distance measure under intuitionistic fuzzy environment. In: Operations Research Forum. Vol. 4(4). Cham: Springer International Publishing; 2023. p. 78

[19] Rani V, Kumar S. Dissimilarity measure between picture fuzzy sets with application to decision-making and medical diagnostic reasoning. In: International Conference on Data Analytics and Insights. Singapore: Springer Nature Singapore; 2023. pp. 767-778

[20] Rani V, Kumar S. An innovative distance measure for quantifying the dissimilarity between q-rung orthopair fuzzy sets. Decision Analytics Journal. 2024;**11**:100440

[21] Arya V, Kumar S. Knowledge measure and entropy: A complementary concept in fuzzy theory. Granular Computing. 2021;**6**(3):631-643

[22] Van Dinh N, Thao NX, Chau NM. Distance and dissimilarity measure of picture fuzzy sets. FAIR. 2017;**10**:104-109

[23] Kumar R, Kumar S. A novel intuitionistic fuzzy similarity measure with applications in decision-making, pattern recognition, and clustering problems. Granular Computing. 2023;**8**(5):1027-1050

[24] Cuong BC, Pham VH. Some fuzzy logic operators for picture fuzzy sets. In: 2015 Seventh International Conference on Knowledge and Systems Engineering (KSE). Ho Chi Minh City, Vietnam: IEEE; 2015. pp. 132-137

[25] Szmidt E, Kacprzyk J. Distances between intuitionistic fuzzy sets. Fuzzy Sets and Systems. 2000;**114**(3):505-518

[26] Wang W, Xin X. Distance measure between intuitionistic fuzzy sets. Pattern Recognition Letters. 2005;**26**(13):2063-2069

[27] Grzegorzewski P. Distances between intuitionistic fuzzy sets and/or interval-valued fuzzy sets based on the Hausdorff metric. Fuzzy Sets and Systems. 2004;**148**(2):319-328

[28] Yang Y, Chiclana F. Consistency of 2D and 3D distances of intuitionistic fuzzy sets. Expert Systems with Applications. 2012;**39**(10):8665-8670

[29] Hwang CL, Yoon KP. Multiple Attribute Decision Making: An Introduction. Sage University Paper Series on Quantitative Applications in the Social Sciences. Thousand Oaks, CA: Sage; 1995. pp. 07-104

[30] Mishra AR, Mardani A, Rani P, Kamyab H, Alrasheedi M. A new intuitionistic fuzzy combinative distance-based assessment framework to assess low-carbon sustainable suppliers in the maritime sector. Energy. 2021;**237**: 121500

[31] Xu Z. Some similarity measures of intuitionistic fuzzy sets and their applications to multiple attribute decision making. Fuzzy Optimization and Decision Making. 2007;**6**:109-121

[32] Wei G. TODIM method for picture fuzzy multiple attribute decision making. Informatica. 2018;**29**(3):555-566

[33] Zhang S, Wei G, Gao H, Wei C, Wei Y. EDAS method for multiple criteria

group decision making with picture fuzzy information and its application to green suppliers selections. Technological and Economic Development of Economy. 2019;**25**(6):1123-1138

[34] Joshi R. A novel decision-making method using R-norm concept and VIKOR approach under picture fuzzy environment. Expert Systems with Applications. 2020;**147**:113228

[35] Chen CT. Extensions of the TOPSIS for group decision-making under fuzzy environment. Fuzzy Sets and Systems. 2000;**114**(1):1-9

[36] Garg H. Some picture fuzzy aggregation operators and their applications to multicriteria decision-making. Arabian Journal for Science and Engineering. 2017;**42**(12):5275-5290